Audrey Fisch's study examines the circulation within England of the people and ideas of the abolitionist campaign. During the 1850s, African-Americans and others active in the campaign to abolish slavery journeyed to England to present the slave experience and rouse opposition to American slavery. Fisch follows the immensely popular campaign as it moved across the Atlantic and intersected with a variety of seemingly unrelated issues: changes in the Victorian literary marketplace; tensions among Victorians about class and gender; anxieties about the integrity of the English character; and questions about the nation's identity. Despite its popular appeal, the African-American abolitionist campaign actually re-energized English nationalism. This book will be of interest to students of African-American studies, and of nineteenth-century American and English literature and history.

AUDREY FISCH is Assistant Professor of English and Co-ordinator of Women's Studies at New Jersey City University. She has published articles and reviews in *Victorian Review*, *Victorian Literature and Culture*, the *Journal of Victorian Culture*, *Nineteenth-Century Contexts*, and *In-Between*. She is co-editor of *The Other Mary Shelley: Beyond Frankenstein*.

AMERICAN SLAVES IN VICTORIAN ENGLAND

Abolitionist Politics in Popular Literature and Culture

AUDREY A. FISCH

CAMBRIDGE
UNIVERSITY PRESS

CAMBRIDGE UNIVERSITY PRESS
Cambridge, New York, Melbourne, Madrid, Cape Town, Singapore,
São Paulo, Delhi, Dubai, Tokyo

Cambridge University Press
The Edinburgh Building, Cambridge CB2 8RU, UK

Published in the United States of America by Cambridge University Press, New York

www.cambridge.org
Information on this title: www.cambridge.org/9780521121651

First published 2000
This digitally printed version 2009

A catalogue record for this publication is available from the British Library

Library of Congress Cataloguing in Publication data

Fisch, Audrey A.
American slaves in Victorian England: abolitionist politics in popular literature and
culture/Audrey A. Fisch.
p. cm.
Includes bibliographical references.
ISBN 0 521 66026 2 (hardback)
1. Antislavery movements – Grest Britain – History – 19th century.
2. Afro-American abolitionists – England – History – 19th century.
3. National characteristics, English – History – 19th century.
4. American literature – 19th century – Appreciation – England.
5. Great Britain – Civilization – American influences. 6. Americans –
Travel – England – History – 19th century. 7. Slavery in literature.
I. Title.
HT1163.F47 1999
326'.8'094209034–dc21
99–22736 CIP

ISBN 978-0-521-66026-6 Hardback
ISBN 978-0-521-12165-1 Paperback

For my grandparents,
Hirsch and Ruth Neuman and Joseph and Adele Fisch

Contents

Acknowledgments

This project would have been endlessly more difficult without the generosity of many, many people. Richard Blackett opened his file cabinets and his home to me; I will never be able to repay to him the debt of thanks that I owe. The genuine intellectual and professional friendship he offered me is rare in academia today; in dark hours, the thought of that generosity sustained me.

Thanks go next to the people who offered friendship and criticism to me while I did research in England, especially Barbara Taylor, Ken Hirschkop, and Sharon Burstyn. Thanks also to the many men (and they were all men) at the Colindale Library who brought me the big dusty binders of old newspapers which would crumble in my fingers.

At home, Rutgers librarians Kevin Mulcahy and Stan Nash found me every obscure reference and newspaper they could, even after I had left Rutgers. Their generosity and knowledge are a credit to their profession.

I would never have survived the ordeal of graduate school and the dissertation without the support and many kind words of Kate Ellis and Donald Gibson. Thanks also to the wonderful help I received from Richard Fulton, Chris Hosgood, and Esther Schor, who guided me through those painful years with savvy advice about academia and wonderful tips about fellowships, publications, and colleagues to contact.

Elise Lemire read every word about ten times and wrote nearly every tenth word. Lisa Botshon was a wonderful editor and friend through much of the revision process. Other support came from Pat Cesarini, Alison Unger, Max Cavitch, Matthew Parr, Lee Joslin, Katie O'Hara, and the Parker Brothers. Jennifer Weintraub, Patricia Moreno, and Ilaria Montagnani assisted in shaping the body of my work and helped to keep me sane.

This project would never have been possible without generous financial support. A Jacob Javits Fellowship gave me the freedom to experiment with a non-traditional dissertation project and to pursue research in England. Research at the Huntington Library was supported by an award from the library in conjunction with the North American Conference on British Studies. A fellowship from the American Association of University Women supported me while I completed the writing. A fellowship from the Center for the Humanities at Wesleyan University and the confidence of Richard Ohmann and Laura Lewis helped me to see how I could transform the dissertation into a book.

Although I received a separately budgeted research grant at New Jersey City University which released me from some of my teaching and allowed me more time to carry out the revisions I needed to do, I am not currently awash in resources for research in my current academic institution. I am, however, sustained by a surfeit of warm, collegial friendships. Thanks go in particular to Doris Friedensohn, Barbara Rubin, David Blackmore, Ellen Garvey, Dexter Marks, and Jo Bruno.

In addition, without the Child Development Center at Giralda Farms, I would never have had time to complete this project. I am lucky to have found a flexible, accommodating day-care center and to have a son, Max Flysch, who likes to sleep.

Thanks also to my parents for supporting my education and respecting my goals. "The Baron Von Shtupnagel" and other stories we shared together over the years taught me to love reading and thinking and inspired me to join a profession where I get to teach others to do the same.

Finally, *à la* Jane Tompkins, I must acknowledge that, beyond all others, I am grateful to Mark Flynn, who has supported me in the most important ways; who gave me criticism even when I stubbornly told him he was stupid and wrong; who gave me hugs and believed in me when I was losing hope; who absorbed my anger and frustrations but never did run anyone over in his car. To him I hope to repay my debt over a lifetime.

Portions of this work appeared earlier, most in substantially different forms, in the following journals, to which I am grateful for the permission to reprint: "'Exhibiting Uncle Tom in Some Shape or Other': The Commodification and Reception of Uncle Tom's Cabin in England," *Nineteenth-Century Contexts* 17.2 (1993): 145–58; "Uncle Tom in England," *Victorian Literature and Culture* 22 (1994): 23–53; "'Repetitious accounts so piteous and so harrowing': The Ideological Work of American Slave Narratives in England," the *Journal of Victorian Culture* 1.1

(Spring 1996): 16–34; and "'Negrophilism' and British Nationalism: The Spectacle of the Black American Abolitionist," *Victorian Review* 19.2 (Winter 1993): 20–47.

Communicating "a correct knowledge of American Slavery": J. B. Estlin and the "breeder" in Frederick Douglass's Narrative

You will understand my feelings (perhaps you may call it fastidious-ness) when I say, that being most desirous to communicate exten-sively a correct knowledge of American Slavery in this city, and rejoicing in having such an excellent opportunity of doing so as Douglass's Narrative furnished me with, I could not circulate it among my friends and especially among ladies (young ones par-ticularly) until I had erased all the paragraphs after the statement that Covey intended the woman be bought for a "*breeder*." The minutia following, that he . . . shut him up with the woman every night for a year, and that the result was twins, are unnecessary and disgusting . . . [such sections would offend] English taste and impede the sale of the book.

(J. B. Estlin to J. Otis, Bristol, 1845)

[Mr. Covey] may be said to have been guilty of compelling his woman slave to commit the sin of adultery. The facts in this case are these: Mr. Covey was a poor man; and he was just commencing in life; he was only able to buy one slave; and, shocking as is the fact, he bought her, as he said for a *breeder* [original emphasis]. This woman was named Caroline. Mr. Covey bought her from Mr. Thomas Lowe, about six miles from St. Michael's. She was a large and able-bodied woman, about twenty years old. She had already given birth to one child, which proved her to be just what he wanted. *After buying her, he hired a married man of Mr. Samuel Harrison, to live with him one year; and him he used to fasten up with her every night! The result was, that, at the end of the year, the miserable woman gave birth to twins. At this result Mr. Covey seemed to be highly pleased, both with the man and the wretched woman. Such was his joy, and that of his wife, that nothing they could do for Caroline during her confinement was too good, or too hard, to be done. The children were regarded as being quite an addition to his wealth.* [The emphasized section here represents the portion of Douglass's text Estlin marked out with X's.]

(Douglass, *Narrative of the Life of Frederick Douglass*, 104–5)

Despite "rejoicing" in the "opportunity" Frederick Douglass's slave narrative provided for disseminating knowledge about the facts of American slavery to English men and women, J. B. Estlin worries about the appropriateness of the text. In particular, the story of how an African-American slave woman was used as a "breeder" distresses Estlin, white abolitionist from Bristol, England. In his letter to his anti-slavery colleague, J. Otis, about his concerns, Estlin expresses his discomfort at the presentation of this incident in the narrative. Estlin seems at least as troubled by Douglass's decision to tell this story of abuse as he is by the sexual abuse itself. Indeed, in the letter, the inclusion of the "breeder" incident within Douglass's narrative serves as the occasion for Estlin to meditate not on American slavery, whatever the facts or the abuse, but on his own anxieties about the English reception and processing of American slavery.

Estlin's anxieties here are far from idiosyncratic. His reaction to Douglass's narrative is in fact symptomatic of the English reception of American abolitionism and of the African-American abolitionist campaign: the letter forms a fascinating micro-example of the concerns and contradictions that structured that reception.

Estlin's reaction to Douglass's book centers around three interrelated areas: the make-up of English audiences/readers (ladies); the quality and discernment of those audiences/readers (English taste); and the commercialism of the abolitionist enterprise (the sale of the book). His remarks are prefaced by his insistence of his allegiance (like every good English abolitionist) to the anti-slavery cause and his unabashed desire to spread the word. Nonetheless, spreading the word raises problems. Estlin's insistence on communicating "correct knowledge" conjures the spectre of knowledge that is somehow not "correct." Does Estlin fear inaccurate information about slavery? Or does his concern about "correct" information mask a desire to ensure that only appropriate, inoffensive ideas be passed along? Concerns about the quality of information transmitted about slavery also give way to questions about those who will receive the information. His remarks about "ladies" (by which term Estlin is certainly excluding working-class women from his purview) suggest that questions about disseminating information about slavery are as much about who should be allowed to hear, read, or know about American slavery as they are about the authentic facts of this system of life and commerce in the United States.

Similarly, Estlin's reference to "English taste" and the question of how the book will sell extends his consideration of not the text itself but its readers. Estlin's insistence that "disgusting" – that is, sexually explicit or explicitly violent – passages might have interfered with the narrative's circulation among ladies and middle- and upper-class men who shared his "English taste" may perhaps be accurate. But considering the fact that sensationalism more and more littered the landscape of Victorian reading material, Estlin's remarks read more as an attempt to reassure himself about his place in the mainstream of Victorian social values than as a reliable description of English taste and reading habits. The growing English desire for titillation in their books and papers, in distinction from Estlin's evocation of English "good" taste, could and often did in fact impel sales of a book.

In other words, Estlin's paternalistic vision of himself as an authoritative judge of information and monitor of what is or is not appropriate for communication betrays a growing perception that such is no longer his role. Indeed, Estlin's remarks belie his inability to oversee who will read Douglass's text and what they will see in the details of those pages. In this light, Estlin's queasiness, his "fastidiousness" about what he at once diminishes as the "minutia" and singles out to condemn as "unnecessary and disgusting" about the text, can be described as a bizarrely myopic attempt at control. Hundreds of passages in Douglass's narrative seem as troublesome as the one Estlin describes. For example, shortly before the section about the "breeder," Douglass describes a master who "Tie[s] up a lame young woman, and whip[s] her with a heavy cowskin upon her naked shoulders, causing the warm red blood to drip" (98–9). Given the existence of many passages like this one in Douglass's narrative, it is surely fair to say that to bowdlerize this text Victorian-style, as Estlin might have wished, would be nearly impossible.

Perhaps for this reason Estlin is specific and focused in his attempt at censorship. Unable to erase the scandals of social and sexual intercourse that the facts of American slavery will betray to a variety of ladies and gentlemen, as well as to Englishmen and women of different classes and tastes, Estlin opts to try to "erase" the "breeder" section, the paragraphs which describe the commercialization of sex for American slaves. In the text of the edition he gave his daughter, Mary Estlin (and in this section alone), Estlin draws bold, strong X's over Frederick Douglass's words.[1]

In circulating Douglass's narrative, as part of a larger effort to inform the English public about American slavery and raise international support for American abolition, Estlin strives for, and is troubled by his lack of, control over a variety of issues seemingly unrelated to the lives of black-skinned men and women across the Atlantic: changes in the Victorian literary marketplace; tensions among Victorians about class and gender; anxieties about the integrity of the English character; changes in the traditional patterns of the consumption of culture; and questions about the nation's identity. Control and authority were increasingly difficult to maintain. "English taste," the pillar of Victorian society, does not necessarily impede the sale of texts with "unnecessary and disgusting" passages, as Estlin wishes. Ladies and others are left vulnerable to, indeed seek out, the "incorrect" knowledge of American slavery, with all its disgusting and disruptive gore and glory. And Estlin cannot erase completely what he does not want others to see. Even in the copy of the text belonging to his daughter, the one person over whom he retained unthreatened authority, Douglass's words remain visible beneath the X's that Estlin uses to mark the offensive passage.

This book, then, is about the dissemination of texts like Douglass's. It is about the reception of these texts, about what they meant to men like Estlin and about what they might have meant to others, like his daughter.

Abolitionism had long been a transatlantic, even an international, phenomenon. Many African-American abolitionists, like Frederick Douglass, participated in the flow of people and ideas that characterized this movement. In his introduction to *The Black Abolitionist Papers*, C. Peter Ripley writes of the several decades of activities of black Americans in England:

> Between 1830 and 1865, black abolitionists left universities, newspaper offices, cabinet shops, pulpits, and plantations for the British Isles. Some boarded the best Cunard Line ships after elaborate farewell gatherings; others sneaked out of American and Canadian harbors just ahead of slave catchers. Many went with the practical and philosophical objectives of the international antislavery movement – spreading the antislavery gospel, building the transatlantic antislavery network, and raising the funds that kept it all going. Others crossed with specific missions, such as raising money to build a church or to purchase a family out of bondage. Fugitive slaves often went to find peace and security – "to live and get a living," as one person described it – leaving, perhaps forever, the threat of southern slave catchers or the persistence of northern racial prejudice . . . They seized any opportunity in the host country to make an antislavery point. (3)

For black Americans in the abolitionist campaign in England, the stakes were fairly clear: personal safety and personal ambition translated readily into public politics.[2] All of this, the journeys and activities of

African-American abolitionists in England, came to a climax in 1850 with the passage of the Fugitive Slave Law, which rendered the Northern states of the US and even Canada unsafe for those fleeing slavery.

After journeying across the Atlantic, these African-Americans found that abolitionism formed a wide arena in which one could both get a living and satisfy one's political goals. Their activities in the abolitionist struggle took several forms: they lectured on their life experiences, circulated slave narratives, displayed enormous panoramas depicting scenes of American slavery, and revealed personal scars and the instruments of torture used in slavery. The presence and activities of the many African-Americans in England from 1850 until the outbreak of the American Civil War form what I am calling the African-American abolitionist campaign.

Whether to purchase narratives, to hear speeches, or to see the authentic scars of slavery on a black man's back, Victorians eagerly paid money and queued up. The African-American abolitionist campaign in England inserted itself into what, most recently, David Turley in *The Culture of English Antislavery, 1780–1860* calls the "long and fluctuating history [of anti-slavery] as a reform cause" (1). Except that this slice of that long history of anti-slavery in England was an immensely popular and commercial campaign that for the first time was structured around the lives, the writings, the presentations, the very bodies of African-Americans.

Following the leads of David Brion Davis, Seymour Drescher, and others,[3] Turley's *The Culture of English Antislavery* focuses on "locating antislavery in a complex picture of the changing economic, social and political order in Britain" (2) and insists on the importance of viewing the anti-slavery movement as "symptomatic of important changes taking place in English culture" (236).[4] The African-American abolitionist campaign was indeed located within a period of change. In particular, the 1850s, with the demise of Chartism and in the aftermath of the "hungry forties," found England reconstructing itself as a glorious nation, prospering in an unprecedented age of progress, and, as a world leader, setting the moral example for nations throughout the globe. Abolitionism was central to this conception of Englishness.[5] From the beginnings of the campaign to abolish colonial English slavery up through the globalization of abolitionism in the mid century, anti-slavery became a "popular outlook on the world" (Turley, *The Culture of English Anti-slavery*, 16). England was the self-declared leader in the fight against the international slave trade (abolished in 1807) and a putatively self-sacrificing, philanthropic nation in its campaign against slavery "at home" in the British colonies (abolished in 1833/8).[6]

But within this same self-congratulating, prosperous nation, other troubles were brewing. While the 1832 Reform Act had legislated only a narrow expansion of political power for the wealthier middle class, the 1850s witnessed the more rapid (and uncontrolled) expansion of cultural power for much of the rest of the population. Amid increasingly shrill concerns about the education and moral taste of the middle and work-ing class and of women, these same groups, in part because of techno-logical advances and in part because of a rise in literacy rates, found themselves with increasing access to, and commercial power over, the circulation of culture (newspapers, high- and low-brow literature, music-hall entertainments, theater, etc.). A new popular order, in other words, threatened the stability of the Victorian social order as new populations began to exert their *de facto* power.

It is into this complicated world of flux and change that Harriet Beecher Stowe's *Uncle Tom's Cabin* entered in 1852, and this forms the subject of my first chapter. Obviously this white New Englander and her sentimental novel form a sharp contrast to the texts, speeches, and personal appearances of African-Americans in the abolitionist cam-paign; Stowe was not Frederick Douglass, and history has judged her and her work very differently. But *Uncle Tom's Cabin* was published in England with unprecedented success, and it commanded an extraordi-nary degree of commercial power. Through the vehicle of the novel, Stowe won the attention of nearly all of the English population and proceeded to cast an indelible image of the American slave on the English imagination: "Uncle Tom" captured the hearts and minds of Victorians as no other fictional or non-fictional character would. In-deed, "Uncle Tom" can be viewed as one of the primary figures of the African-American abolitionist campaign, despite his only fictional exist-ence. For all these reasons, Stowe's text set the terms of debate for abolitionism in England in the decade of the 1850s.

To flesh out the terms of that debate, I consider reviews of Stowe's novel in the Victorian periodical press. The responses to *Uncle Tom's Cabin* make clear that Stowe's novel raised many of the same concerns that bothered Estlin about Frederick Douglass's narrative. In particular, reactions betray anxiety about "the people," whose vulnerability is exemplified by their susceptibility to the irrational and irresponsible appeal of Stowe's novel. Given the "uncultivated" readers dominating the newly emerging reading public, reviewers wondered how standards of truth and beauty in literature would withstand the assault of sub-standard texts like *Uncle Tom's Cabin*. Furthermore, such fears about the consequences of the English reader's exposure to and defenselessness against political propaganda, such as Stowe's text, had implications beyond the realm of the literary. Questions of whether or not an English "lady" would find acceptable a seemingly disgusting passage or of whether or not a working-class reader would be manipulated by Stowe's purportedly illogical ideas translated, more grandly, into a question about weakness or degradation within the nation's character.

In other words, *Uncle Tom's Cabin* served as the ground on which a range of issues within mid-Victorian England were argued and debated: questions about culture, gender, class, and national identity. Abolitionism served as a sounding board used both to expose changes in mid-Victorian society and to contain and control the implications and ramifications of those changes. Again, Estlin identifies Douglass's narrative as a threat to the traditions of English taste and virtue, and he attempts with the excision of one passage to ward off the encroachment symbolized by the circulation of Douglass's narrative. And Estlin's was not a unique reaction; it is symptomatic of a more general response.

Shortly after the publication of Stowe's novel, a self-described sequel to *Uncle Tom's Cabin* appeared, published anonymously in 1852 in England. The subject of my second chapter, *Uncle Tom in England* is clearly an attempt to speak to and assuage the concerns raised by the publication and massive circulation of *Uncle Tom's Cabin*. It also clearly aimed to displace Stowe's "Uncle Tom" and to combat all that he had come to mean to Victorians by introducing a new fictional "Uncle Tom." Re-writing, then, both fiction and history, *Uncle Tom in England* delivers a conservative and fiercely nationalist translation for Victorians of the issues raised by American abolitionism generally, by the fictional "Uncle Tom," and by African-American abolitionists. The novel yokes together American abolitionism and Chartism, the working-class movement for universal male suffrage, but not to engineer a campaign for universal justice or a recognition of the links between different systems of social oppression. Instead the novel manages to produce a full-scale discrediting of the values of Chartism, a commemoration of the history of English reform, and a heightening of English national chauvinism. Erasing or suppressing English internal differences (about the unrealized goals of Chartism or the plight of women piece-workers, for example), *Uncle Tom in England* concludes that England will, followed by the United States, lead the nations of the world on the path of moral and economic progress. The evidence of dissonance and vulnerability within the English populace exposed by the success of Stowe's novel and excoriated in the responses to it is re-cast; like Estlin, *Uncle Tom in England* seeks to contain and control abolitionism and to impart its version of "correct knowledge."

While this new fictional "Uncle Tom" was struggling to supplant Stowe's character, however, non-fictional, flesh-and-blood ex-slaves and free-born black men and women were also struggling to convey their ideas without being either crushed under fictional images or censored by Victorian fastidiousness. The second half of this book turns to these struggles and examines how the texts and personalities of "real" African-Americans were consumed in English society.

The widespread circulation of African-Americans on the lecture circuit and of their narratives in the literary marketplace worried the Victorian press for many of the same reasons that *Uncle Tom's Cabin* was perceived as a peril. It signalled the success of a new cultural economy in which the reader's uncultivated, even degraded demands for the previously illicit – sex, violence, and entertainment – might prevail. The popularity of the African-American abolitionist campaign implied that men like Estlin could no longer cross out a single passage of a text and feel assured of the stability of their cherished values. But while the African-American abolitionist campaign acted as a catalyst for the formation of a series of difficult questions about changing values, changing tastes, and a changing nation, it also provided a resolution to the very challenges these questions posed. The Victorian reader's or spectator's voyeuristic interest in American slavery could, for example, be recuperated: re-defined as the philanthropic and noble interest of a superior nation called to witness the degradation of American society. In other words, growing anxieties about the power and prurience of the English people, and about the identity of the English nation, were agitated but also resolved by these abolitionist texts and events.

My third chapter examines the reception of American slave narratives, focusing in particular on American ex-slave John Brown's narrative, *Slave Life in Georgia*, and on responses to Brown's text from the English press. The level of anxiety surrounding the circulation of slave narratives bears witness to their power to unsettle men like Estlin and to their subversive potential. In part because it remains difficult to recover actual Victorian reading experiences of these texts, it is impossible to prove whether the narratives actually escaped the damaging censorship exemplified by Estlin's attempts to excise Douglass's narrative and by

Uncle Tom in England's efforts to re-construct and thus stymie the transgressive potential of "Uncle Tom." In the final section of his narrative, Brown attempts to tell the story of the complicated intersections of national culpability in one slave's life. This piece of his narrative, however, seems to have gone unread or at least unnoticed by Victorian reviewers (and Victorian readers?) and in no way interferes with the construction of his life as typical product of the transatlantic campaign, malleable to the English public's needs. Read instead within the context of anxieties about the demand-controlled economy of the literary marketplace in which degraded texts such as slave narratives can thrive, John Brown's narrative is both appropriated as an icon of the degradation of the English literary marketplace and, at the very same time, read as a testament to English national superiority in contrast to degraded, slavery-infected America. Thus the text is used to disarm the very anxieties it raises and inevitably serves as an affirmation of the greatness of English national identity. It does not seem to have provoked, as Brown probably intended it to, a challenge to that national greatness.

My fourth chapter examines the presence and impact of the antislavery lecture tours conducted by so many African-American abolitionists. I concentrate on two contrasting figures, Henry "Box" Brown and Sarah Parker Remond. "Box" Brown was the showman of the lecture circuit, his buffoonery interpreted in various ways in the press as evidence of the backwardness of American society. The cultured and light-skinned Remond, the only woman active on the lecture circuit, constituted a different kind of spectacle: the debasement of a Lady by slavery and American society. In both cases, their presence on the lecture platform served as illustrations of American society as an exotic and degraded "other" against which English nationalism could define and extol itself. Henry "Box" Brown and Sarah Remond resisted this appropriation however; and each struggled to define a public persona which was not an easy lackey to English national desires for self-sanctification. For "Box" Brown, the struggle involved a lawsuit against an English newspaper editor who had tried to shut down "Box" Brown's show and hence had interfered with his profits. For Remond, the struggle meant resisting an alliance with the white middle- and upper-class women in her audiences who were eager to identify with her and to single out the potential abuse of women like her as the abominable crime of slavery. Instead, Remond tried to evoke for her audiences her sisterhood with the ordinary, uneducated, abused slave woman, whom she represented, for whom she hoped to earn respect and freedom, and with whom Victorian women could not easily sympathize or identify. Perhaps more than John Brown, "Box" Brown and Remond succeeded in achieving independent voices. But both also found it difficult to refrain from reverting back to the parts written for them in the larger drama of American abolition in England in which they had always been cast.

The African-American abolitionist campaign in England, a phenomenon grounded in the politics of abolition but infused with the energy of popular appeal, was an event with enormous possibilities for radical change. Political potential, however, neither guarantees nor describes political effect. As the black American abolitionist campaign was translated across the Atlantic, it was manipulated into pre-existing Victorian discourses of culture and class, the worker/slave, education and exotica, and became a compelling touchstone for English nationalism. The African-American abolitionist campaign worked its way through those debates, but what emerged was not a progressive alignment of English and American reform causes (of, for example, white English workers and black American slaves) but the retrenchment of social and cultural values and the emergence of a newly energized English nationalism. Still, gaps and fissures in the neat façade of the African-American abolitionist campaign's absorption into English society suggest that not everything was as tightly or perfectly controlled as some might have liked. It is, I think, fascinating to consider the ways in which the dangers of abolitionism, and of what abolitionism threatened to expose about Victorian society itself, were met at every pass and eagerly contained and contested. That is the subject of this study. What remain equally interesting, although less accessible, are the ways in which that control was never total. John Estlin could neither erase the offending "breeder" section nor stem the circulation of Frederick Douglass's text.

CHAPTER I

"Exhibiting Uncle Tom in some shape or other": the commercialization and reception of Uncle Tom's Cabin in England

This picture of life in the Slave States of America undoubtedly owes some of its interest to the novelty of its subject. Manners, domestic economy, sketches of scenery, and "interiors," which if drawn in England would attract little attention although equally well done, have the charm of freshness when displaying a state of society which is sufficiently removed from our own to be new yet not so remote as to be strange. If, however, these advantages were put aside, *Uncle Tom's Cabin* would still be very remarkable as an artistic production, whether considered merely as a romance or as a didactic fiction.

("Uncle Tom's Cabin," *Spectator*, 926)

So begins a review[1] of *Uncle Tom's Cabin* carried on September 25, 1852, in the *Spectator*.[2] Harriet Beecher Stowe's novel is praised both as "romance," on the grounds of its artistic merits, and as "didactic fiction," on the grounds of its abolitionist politics. The review goes on to tell English readers that Stowe's novel "has produced a great sensation in America" (928) and confidently asserts that the popularity of the novel in England, "equally great," is the result in part of English interest in the charming freshness of American society.[3]

A notice of a theatrical production of Stowe's novel carried on December 4, 1852, in the same journal offers an entirely different opinion. Under the heading "The Theatres," the notice begins with an argument showing "that both form and substance preclude *Uncle Tom's Cabin* from anything like adequate representation on the stage" (1160). Despising the production of a stage version at the Adelphi Theatre, the review insists sarcastically that "No one has more clearly seen than the authors of the Adelphi *Uncle Tom* the utter unfitness of the story for the

A version of this chapter was presented at the Research Society for Victorian Periodicals conference, 1992, and I am grateful to the session chair, Laurel Brake, and the participants for their helpful comments. For encouragement and patient criticism of this piece, I would also like to thank Richard Fulton, Claire Berardini, Elise Lemire, and Mark Flynn.

stage" (1160). These authors have altered, re-invented, and transposed the novel and "have succeeded in working out a perfectly inoffensive drama, of considerable constructive merit," but "Not one of the qualities which strike the heart in Mrs. Stowe's novel is preserved in this play" (1160).

This notice continues, however, and it is not this particular inadequate version of Stowe's novel that dominates the reviewer's concerns. It is, instead, the wholesale, uncultured consumption by "the mob" (1160) of this commercialized *Uncle Tom's Cabin* which upsets and provokes the *Spectator*. The reviewer writes that "the mob," Victorian shorthand for the working class, those without education and cultural taste, having "read a popular book," are "rushing to see the leading personages placed in a visible shape before its eyes. Nearly all those theatres which stand below the level of dramatic criticism have attracted crowds by exhibiting Uncle Tom in some shape or other; and now – somewhat late in the day – the Adelphi joins the throng [of] Tommania" (1160). Greedily and vulgarly consumed by the objectified and de-humanized "throng" of the "mob," *Uncle Tom's Cabin* is transformed in the very same journal from a popular American romance or didactic fiction to an unwitting (at least in this account) player in an English drama of cultural crisis in which the theater, one facet of that Arnoldian Culture to which Victorian society aspired, is threatened by the uncultured mob.[4]

Witting or unwitting, the participation of *Uncle Tom's Cabin* in this Victorian drama shaped the novel's reception. In order to understand this dynamic and its effect on the English reception of *Uncle Tom's Cabin*, we need to turn back to the history of the English publication and commercialization of Stowe's novel.

Shortly after the novel's publication in the United States on March 20, 1852, an employee at the New York publishing house of Putnam's mailed a two-volume set of *Uncle Tom's Cabin* to a contact in England. As early as July 8, 1852, following the custom of transatlantic literary piracy common for the day, several English publishers began to bring out editions of the novel. "After lying dormant on the bookstalls for several weeks," Forrest Wilson writes in *Crusader in Crinoline*, his biography of Harriet Beecher Stowe, "the novel all at once exploded into popular favour, as half a dozen London publishers, discovering that the text was unprotected, brought out their editions simultaneously" (302). The *Morning Chronicle* writes of "illustrated editions, and newspaper printed editions, and editions in parts and numbers," concluding that *Uncle Tom's Cabin* is "the book of the day" and its "circulation . . . a thing unparalleled in bookselling annals." The *Eclectic Review* records the novel's "marvellous popularity" (720–1): "its sale has vastly exceeded that of any other work in any other age or country" (720); *Blackwood's Edinburgh Magazine* describes "the sale of *Uncle Tom's Cabin*" as "the most marvellous literary phenomenon that the world has witnessed" ("Uncle Tom's Cabin," 393).[5]

The "general hubbub raised in England by Harriet's novel" (Wilson, *Crusader*, 327) soon extended to the full-scale commercialization of *Uncle Tom's Cabin*. The *Spectator* offered a name for this phenomenon of commercialization, as noted above: "Tom-mania" ("The Theatres," 1160).[6] "The extraordinary enthusiasm for Uncle Tom could not be satisfied by [a] simple reading of the novel," writes Douglas A. Lorimer in his *Colour, Class, and the Victorians*.

Publishers, shopkeepers, and enterprising manufacturers soon set out to capitalize on this "Uncle Tom-mania" . . . Songbooks appeared with fulsome illustrations of famous passages in the novel. Wallpaper depicting Uncle Tom and Topsy in characteristic poses, or Eliza and Harry's famous escape, began to cover nursery walls. Uncle Tom mementos and ornaments cluttered curio shops, and Topsy dolls won the tender care and affection of little English Eva. (85)

There were also paintings of "Uncle Tom and Cassy" and "Eva's Farewell" by Royal Academicians, and panoramas, giant narrative paintings with several frames depicting various poignant moments from the novel. In 1853, *The Uncle Tom's Cabin Almanack or Abolitionist Memento* was published with twenty-seven illustrations by George Cruikshank for those who wished the everyday use of "an inseparable companion" to have "a daily lesson about and to bear a daily witness" to the cause of abolition and to Uncle Tom (4). A card game, "a set of 'Uncle Tom Quadrilles,'" was pronounced by the *Prospective Review* to be "the delight of the approaching season" (491).

Theatrical troupes travelled the country performing popular scenes from the novel. By December 1852, the English stage "was crowded with eleven different competing dramatizations" of the novel (Birdoff, *The World's Greatest Hit*, 144), and by Christmas of that year four Uncle Tom pantomimes had appeared (Lorimer, *Colour*, 86). Just as the theaters "riva[l] each other in efforts to invest [*Uncle Tom's Cabin*] with dramatic interest," the *Eclectic Review* notes: "The harmonies of song [are] used to convey its sentiments to the heart" (721). Songs included

"The Little Evangelist," "Poor Uncle Tom," "The Slave Wife," "Eva," "The Fugitive Slave," "Emmeline," and "A Tear for Uncle Tom" (Wilson, *Crusader*, 327).

Some Tom-mania products were attached to explicit anti-slavery politics. Anti-slavery notepaper, for example, picturing Tom with small Eva and the caption " 'These things sink into my heart Uncle Tom,' said Eva," was sold as part of the penny offering organized by the women of England to collect money for Harriet Beecher Stowe to administer in the cause of American abolition. But the visage of "Uncle Tom" was also used to sell a variety of products in no way related to abolitionism. As Harry Birdoff records:

All along the London streets the wagons of retail shops rumbled on, carrying Tom's face on placards, and named after him were a great variety of articles: "Uncle Tom's pure unadulterated coffee," "Uncle Tom's improved flagelots," "Uncle Tom china," "Uncle Tom's paletot," "Uncle Tom's new and second-hand clothing," "Uncle Tom's shrinkable woolen stockings" . . . Named after the humble abode of Uncle Tom were many creameries and eating places, pastry shops, dry-goods emporiums, and cameo shops. (*The World's Greatest Hit*, 144–5)

Uncle Tom's Cabin, as Marcus Wood writes, was "a publishing and merchandising phenomenon" ("Uncle Tom in England," 83).

From within this "hubbub" of "Tom-mania," it is difficult to separate out the strains of politics and capitalism. However, the fact that the consumption by Victorians of "Uncle Tom" in his various commercial forms was nearly universal is clear. The *Nonconformist* remarks that *Uncle Tom's Cabin* "is in voracious demand among all classes – the book peeps out from the apron, lies beside the workman at his bench, and is found on every drawing-room table" ("Uncle Tom's Cabin," 708). Likewise, the *Eclectic Review* emphasizes that the novel "has found its way to the extremes of society, and its effect everywhere is the same. In the palace, the mansion, and the cottage, it has rivetted attention. The sons of toil as well as the children of opulence have wept over its pages" (720). The review continues, recording what it considers the "notorious" fact "that men of all classes, persons of every conceivable grade, the mechanic and the manufacturer, peers and rustics, literary men and children, lawyers, physicians and divines, members of both sexes, of every age, and of all conceivable varieties of disposition, have perused its touching narrative with moistened eye and with agonized heart" (720). The same depth and breadth may be ascribed to the consumption of "Uncle Tom" in his other forms: the working-class man enjoyed "Tom" in the form of circulating panoramas while the woman of leisure enjoyed him in her daily almanack. Like the anti-slavery cause itself, the consumption of "Uncle Tom" travelled across political lines, from the wallpaper sensationalizing the escape of Harry and Eliza to the overtly reformist anti-slavery notepaper funding the penny offering.

The *Prospective Review* makes an important point about the technological and social advances which made possible the unprecedented success of the novel: "Everything conspires to make the success of Mrs. Stowe one of the most remarkable on record in the recent history of English literature; the progress of the cheap printing movement; the facilities of communication; the absence of any English copyright" (491). Also recognizing the technological and social advances that made the particular commodification of Stowe's novel possible, John Ross Dix writes:

"Uncle Tom" is not only a miracle of itself, but it announces the commencement of a miraculous era in the literary world . . . Such a phenomenon as its present popularity [indicates] could have happened only in the present wondrous age. It required all the aid of our new machinery to produce the phenomenon; our steam presses, steam-ships, steam-carriages, iron roads, electric telegraphs, and universal peace among the reading nations of the earth. But beyond all, it required the readers to consume the books, and these have never before been so numerous . . . the great avenues of literature are all open, wide, and well paved, and free to all who have the strength to travel in them. Hereafter, the book which does not circulate to the extent of a million copies will be regarded as a failure. (*Transatlantic Tracings*, 70)

For many, however, the images conjured here by Dix were nothing to celebrate: the permeation of Victorian culture by "Uncle Tom" was "notorious," as the *Eclectic Review* put it, rather than miraculous. The unprecedented commercialization of the novel gave Stowe's text unparalleled power. As much in response to this new commercial phenomenon which *Uncle Tom's Cabin* had inaugurated in the world of Victorian culture as to the thematics of the novel itself, voices of intellectual, moral, literary, and political doubt emerged. These voices of doubt reverberated around issues in Victorian society for which *Uncle Tom's Cabin* became an unlikely sounding board. By studying these reactions, many published in the form of reviews of the novel,[7] we gain access not to the precise meaning of *Uncle Tom's Cabin* or "Tom-mania" for Victorians, nor to the meaning of the African-American abolitionist campaign for Victorian society generally, but to the constellation of

Victorian social concerns assigned to this cultural event and worried over in the nineteenth-century press.[8]

The long, four-column review of *Uncle Tom's Cabin* which appeared in *The Times* on Friday, September 3, 1852, is crucial for our understanding of the meanings Stowe's text acquired for English readers, both because it exemplifies the hysteria Stowe's novel produced in the press and elsewhere and because this highly influential review (in a highly influential paper) articulated the terms of debate on which much further discussion of the text would depend.[9] The agitation underlying *The Times*'s review, as we shall see, is commensurate not so much with Stowe's text as an abolitionist document *per se* but with the anxieties underlying Victorian questions about the definition and role of culture, of the expanding reading public, and about working-class revolt, Victorian questions for which Stowe's text became a touchstone. It is around these questions, current pressure points within Victorian society, that the reviewer focuses his attention (and it is likely to have been *his*).

While the review begins with the concession that Stowe's novel "is a decided hit," adding that "It is impossible not to feel respect for *Uncle Tom's Cabin*," *The Times* insists that, for two reasons, there is very little to praise about this novel. First, the reviewer cites with disdain figures from the *Boston Traveller* which establish the financial excesses of *Uncle Tom's Cabin*: "the authoress has already received from her publishers the sum of '$10,300 as her copy-right premium on three months' sales of the work, – we believe the largest sum of money ever received by any author, either American or European, from the sales of a single work in so short a period of time.'"[10] Second, the review disparages the novel on account of the gender of its author: "Able as she is, Mrs. Stowe . . . will suffer in the minds of the judicious from the female error. With so good a cause it is a pity that her honest zeal should have outrun discretion." Yet the flaws of Stowe's works are less the result of her indiscretion than they are the inevitable fault of her gender: "With the instinct of [a] beginner the clever authoress takes the shortest road to her purpose, and strikes at the convictions of her readers by assailing their hearts . . . Who shall deny to a true woman the use of her true weapons?" Inevitably, the woman writer uses the weapons of her gender, such as "assailing [the] hearts" of her readers, yet with these weapons discredited as improper and with the equation of "woman writer" with "erring beginner" neatly in place, *The Times* is "content to warn the unsuspecting reader." Reader beware: this grotesquely commercial novel is built out of the wiliness of women and their unscrupulous weapons.[11]

With these indictments of the novel in place, the notice proceeds to deny the political efficacy of Stowe's novel:

> that [Stowe] will help in the slightest degree towards the removal of the gigantic evil that afflicts her soul is a matter upon which we may express the greatest doubt: nay, is a matter upon which, unfortunately, we have very little doubt at all, inasmuch as we are certain that the very readiest way to rivet the fetters of slavery in these critical times is to direct against all slaveholders in America the opprobrium and indignation which such works as *Uncle Tom's Cabin* are sure to excite.

If Stowe's novel is not only unlikely to aid the abolitionist cause, but also likely to confound that cause, it is worth asking why this politically inefficient woman's novel is singled out for such lengthy and detailed analysis in *The Times*. Is the review disingenuous in its expression of "very little doubt" that *Uncle Tom's Cabin* will not "in the slightest degree" help remove slavery from the United States or in its dismissal of Stowe's authorship on the grounds of gender? Or is this review merely begrudged to Stowe's novel because of its unprecedented popularity? The answer lies partly in *The Times*'s antipathy to American abolitionism: the review of Stowe's abolitionist novel serves as a political opportunity to discredit "the cause."[12] Beyond such partisan behavior, however, lies the fact that *The Times* is very much afraid of the political consequences of Stowe's novel, the difference her text might make through its wiles, weapons, and its sheer power for *English* audiences. In particular, *The Times*'s antipathy stems from a larger gender- and class-based fear. As we shall see, the review worries about the novel's ability to "excite" the "opprobrium and indignation" of "unsuspecting" readers not only against the injustice of slavery but against the unjust power relations on which slavery and other systems of oppression are based. Furthermore, as its popularity increases, the chances for Stowe's novel to make that difference would seem to increase exponentially.

These underlying anxieties structure *The Times*'s argument with Stowe's portrayal of the condition and plight of blacks in American slavery. The argument is introduced by a note of congratulation towards Stowe on her honest depictions: "We know no book in which the negro character finds such successful interpretation, and appears so life-like and so fresh." Congratulation gives way to complaint, however, as *The Times* denounces the inauthenticity of Stowe's portrayals: for example, Tom "walk[s] through the world with a Bible in his hands, and virtuous indignation on his lips . . . eternally playing for our edification and moral improvement." It is the inaccuracy of such character sketches, according to *The Times*, which troubles the book's political project:

Before we export another white enthusiast from Exeter-hall, let us import a dozen or two blacks to teach Exeter-hall its most obvious Christian duties. If Mrs. Stowe's portraiture is correct, and if Uncle Tom is a type of a class, we deliberately assert that we have nothing more to communicate to the negro, but everything to learn from his profession and practice.

The practices of English imperial philanthropy, represented here by "Exeter-hall"[13] and associated with Christianity, function as synecdoches for civilization, with its firmly established hierarchies of religion and race. The review here associates Stowe's deliberately positive and thereby radical "portraiture" of "African nature" with the complete overturning of the hierarchies of civilization: "In her very eagerness to accomplish her amiable intention, Mrs. Stowe ludicrously stumbles and falls very far short of her object. She should surely have contented herself with proving the infamy of the slave system, and not been tempted to establish the superiority of the African nature over that of the Anglo-Saxon and of every other known race." Placing Stowe's claim that virtue exists in the "African nature" in the context of such complete political and social upheaval, *The Times* can easily ridicule Stowe and swiftly dismiss her claims.

As if the obvious superiority of "every other known race" to the African nature was not argument enough against Stowe's project, the review continues to take issue with Stowe by insisting that she "has certainly not done justice to" the subject of the condition of blacks in slavery. Approaching the tinder box of comparison between American slaves and the English working class, *The Times* manipulates English national chauvinism and racism to make its case. "The general condition of the southern slaves," *The Times* insists, is "one of comparative happiness and comfort, such as many a free man in the united kingdom [*sic*] might regard with envy." On this subject, *The Times* quotes William Thomson, a Scottish weaver who had travelled in the United States and who "asserted that he had never beheld one-fifth of the real suffering [among slaves] that he had seen among the labouring poor in England," and that "the members of the same family of negroes are not so much scattered as are those of working men in Scotland, whose necessities compel them to separate at an age when the American slave is running about gathering health and strength." The comparison of the plight of the black slave with that of the white laborer is maneuvered so as to strike the final blow to Stowe's credibility. Obviously, nationalism and racism combine here to cement the identification of the white English reader of any class with his suffering light-skinned, Anglo-Saxon, Scottish brother over and against the comfortable black American slave (albeit "a man and a brother"). Moreover, for working-class readers, or readers with sympathies in that direction, this allusion to the previous competition between English laborers and black slaves is designed to ensure that sympathy is turned away from Stowe and from her portrait of the American black. The mathematical comparison of ratios of suffering, the white laborer suffering five times more than the black slave, plays on a history of discussions of the hypocritical concern on the part of the middle- and upper-class English for the plight of West Indian blacks at the expense of England's laboring poor (England's white slaves).[14]

If *The Times*, however, can easily dismiss Stowe's inaccurate portrayal of blacks and the novel's claims on English sympathy for the cause of abolitionism, *Uncle Tom's Cabin* remains dangerous because, according to *The Times*, Stowe's text doesn't function as literature ought to. Concerns here about how literature should and should not function must be understood within the context of the expansion of the reading public, due to an increase in literacy and to changes in printing technology, in the first half of the nineteenth century.[15]

As new and different reading material became cheaper and more available, critics feared that middle-class readers, particularly women, were vulnerable to the threat of degraded reading matter. Concern about threats from the new literary marketplace to the taste and cultivation of middle-class readers, however, paled in comparison with anxiety about working-class readers. Richard Altick notes: "there was deep (and not wholly idle) apprehension that making the 'lower ranks' of society literate would breed all sorts of disorder and debauchery" (*The English Common Reader*, 5). An observer at a meeting for the Society for the Promotion of Christian Knowledge is recorded to have said, in 1832, that "The population of this country [was] for the first time becoming a *reading* population, actuated by tastes and habits unknown to preceding generations, and particularly susceptible to such an influence as that of the press" (qtd. in L. James, *English Popular Literature*, 18).

In his later *Culture and Anarchy*, Matthew Arnold alludes to one form of reaction from the middle and upper classes in the 1830s and 1840s to the threat of "disorder" among a newly literate but "susceptible" working class:

Plenty of people . . . give the masses, as they call them, an intellectual food prepared and adapted in the way they think proper for the actual condition of the masses. The ordinary popular literature is an example of this way of working on the masses. Plenty of people will try to indoctrinate the masses with the set of ideas and judgments constituting the creed of their own profession or party. (69–70)

Arnold, himself an Inspector of Schools, concedes to popular literature here a large degree of power for "working on the masses" and worries over the proper administration of that power. Arnold's anxieties exemplify what Richard Johnson has described as the "Victorian obsession with the education of the poor": "a concern about authority, about power, about the assertion (or the re-assertion?) of control [and] an attempt to determine, through the capture of educational means, the patterns of thought, sentiment and behavior of the working class" ("Educational Policy," 119).[16]

Since the distribution of tracts to the poor and the control of poor and charitable educational institutions were so often attempts to infiltrate and manipulate the working classes, the same infiltration by *Uncle Tom's Cabin*, achieved with unexpected success, raised many Victorian hackles. Did Stowe's novel represent the "education" by indoctrination that Arnold identified: the attempt to use popular literature "to raise a new race of working people – respectful, cheerful, hard-working, loyal, pacific, and religious" (Johnson, "Educational Policy," 119)? Or did *Uncle Tom's Cabin* represent the "popular literature" already consumed by the working class, "obscene, exciting, and irreligious works" (106) which threatened to perpetuate degraded and uncivilized working-class behavior?[17]

Within the context of anxiety about the expansion of the reading public and plans for the manipulation and "transformation" of the working classes through education, *The Times*'s concerns about how Stowe's text operates to corrupt its readers become more clear. For one thing, the widespread popularity of *Uncle Tom's Cabin* guaranteed that "rational thinkers," those presumed by *The Times* to be educated or cultured enough to be aware of how they were being manipulated by the irresponsible weapons of a woman writer, would be a minority within the audience for the novel. The rest of the audience, not already educated and cultured, were unlikely, according to *The Times*, to receive the proper instruction they needed in steady, rational justice from the likes of Stowe:

> She cannot hold the scales of justice with a steady hand, but she has learnt to perfection the craft of the advocate. *Euclid*, she well knows, is no child for effecting social revolutions, but an impassioned song may set a world in conflagration . . . Perhaps there is, after all, but one method of carrying on a crusade, and that unscrupulous fighting is the rightful warfare of the crusader.

Not only does Stowe's writing represent "unscrupulous . . . warfare," but it is a warfare against which *The Times* fears many of its readers will be defenseless. Recall the earlier suggestion that "such works as *Uncle Tom's Cabin* are sure to excite [opprobrium and indignation]." These texts "excite," as opposed to educating or enlightening, their readers. *The Times* insists that:

> Let the attempt be made imperiously and violently to dictate to the south, and from that hour the Union is at an end . . . The writer of *Uncle Tom's Cabin* and similar well-disposed authors have yet to learn that to excite the passions of their readers in favour of their philanthropic schemes is the very worst mode of getting rid of a difficulty [namely, slavery, which is] part and parcel of the whole social organization . . . and cannot be forcibly removed without instant anarchy, and all its accompanying mischief.

Stowe's novel, by calculating to "excite the passions" of the reader, in turn threatens to undermine the social status quo, to undo the union of the United States, and to "set [the] world in conflagration." Substantive issues, such as whether Stowe is accurate in her portrayal of blacks in American slavery, are no longer at stake here; instead, what *The Times* stresses is the manner in which *Uncle Tom's Cabin* works on and corrupts its readers, leading them to a dangerous state of excitement approaching anarchy.

A cursory look at the novel's structure confirms, for an increasingly anxious reviewer, that not only does the novel not function as literature ought to, but that it is not "Literature":

> Her narrative is rather a succession of detached scenes than a compact, well-jointed whole, and many of the scenes are tedious from their similarity and repetition. The reader is interested in the fate of two heroes, but their streams of adventure never blend. The scene closes upon Uncle Tom to open upon George Harris, and it closes upon George Harris to open upon Uncle Tom, – a style of proceeding well understood at the Adelphi Theatre . . . but certainly not yet recognized in the classic realms of art.

The dramatic, non-literary style of the novel may in fact explain its popularity with those newly literate readers whose tastes have developed at the Adelphi Theatre,[18] not in the universities.

However, relegating *Uncle Tom's Cabin* to the realm of popular drama, well beneath the classic domains of "Art," does not dispose of the anxiety surrounding its popularity and its ability, consequently, to wield its weapons. *The Times* can only hope that Victorian common sense will prevail over Stowe's devices: "common sense and a feeling of what is due to our better nature will assuredly prevent all but the veriest fanatics from accepting as truth such exaggerated and unholy fables." At the same time, the review worries about those readers whose "better natures" may be undeveloped because of their lack of education or culture:

What becomes of the judgment . . . if the intellect be weak and the heart be strong? We are not ignorant of the mode in which great morals are enforced at our minor theatres, and of the means there taken to impress the imagination and to instruct the intellect by help of the domestic melodrama . . . It is very easy to educe startling lessons from a dramatic work, as it is easy enough for an artist to delineate fear by painting a man with staring eyes, open mouth, and hair on end. Truth, however, demands more delicate dealing, and art that would interpret Truth must watch the harmonies of Nature, which charms not by great "effect," but by her blended sympathy and grace, by her logical and unforced developments. Did we know nothing of the subject treated by Mrs. Stowe, we confess that we should hesitate before accepting much of her coin as sterling metal.

Like the review's insistence that *Uncle Tom's Cabin* is a politically ineffic-ient woman's novel, in the midst of a lengthy detailed analysis, there is a contradiction lying at the heart of all this grand rhetoric. On the one hand, *The Times* insists that Stowe ought not to be paid attention to, that her work is unlikely to make a difference, that it fails to convince, and that her false metals are not likely to be mistook for "sterling," that is, good, sound English coin. On the other hand, the notice worries that Stowe is likely to excite "opprobrium" and "indignation" which might tend to imperious and violent behavior such as the disruption of the Union or worse, that her novel "educe[s] startling lessons" and may, like melodrama, "enforce" by "impress[ing] the imagination" and "in-struct[ing] the intellect." While it ought to be ignored, her novel may succeed in its work; *The Times* despairs at this thought.

This contradiction leads us to the very heart of the threat of the novel: that it will inevitably succeed in "enforcing" and "impressing" its incorrect message on the many "weak intellects" and "strong hearts" of *its poorly educated readers. The Times* writes: "Its very popularity constitutes its greatest difficulty. It will keep ill-blood at boiling point [*sic*], and irritate instead of pacifying those whose proceedings Mrs. Stowe is anxious to influence on behalf of humanity." Indeed, the female-authored novel succeeds in making men "excitable," subject to the tempers and irritations of the blood, infecting them, as it were, with the hysteria customarily associated with women. The problem, for *The Times*, seems to be not so much with *Uncle Tom's Cabin* but with the existence of vulnerable readers who could be duped by this "clever authoress."[19]

I suggested earlier that *The Times's* review exemplifies a hysterical English reaction to *Uncle Tom's Cabin*, a reaction to the Victorian questions for which Stowe's text became a touchstone in part because of the unique commercialization of the text, the phenomenon of "Tommania." Unpacked, *The Times's* loaded response reveals anxieties about the newly emerging Victorian "common reader" (to borrow Richard Altick's term), about the newly emerging literary marketplace, and about what changes these portend for both social and literary hierarchies.

The Times's review was not simply one among many opinions; a powerful cultural force in mid-Victorian England, *The Times* was capable of creating and setting the terms of critical debate for a cultural event. In this instance, *The Times* typifies what Stuart Hall describes as the press's ability to shape as well as represent public opinion:

The press "represents" the opinions of the people to the state. These opinions do not, however, exist outside the process and the means of representation. Representation is a two-way process. For example, in the process of articulating public opinion, the press . . . helps to form "public opinion" – in the simplest sense by formulating it. We know better what we think, and have a clearer sense of our interests when we see them formulated in the public domain, in a public language, on our behalf. ("Culture and the State," 19)[20]

A letter to the editor of *The Times*, appearing on September 7, 1852, illustrates Hall's point. The letter is interesting for the way it duplicates the terms of cultural crisis featured in *The Times's* review and thus demonstrates "the public language" of the debate around *Uncle Tom's Cabin*. Agreeing that Stowe's text "is overdrawn far beyond the limit even of novel-writing," the writer worries, with *The Times*, about the effect of this novel and this kind of writing on readers. "A Constant Reader" continues:

I fear that the book will raise the jests of the profane, and the sneers of those whom we most want to bring round to our party. It will be immortalized at the

Victoria and Bower Saloon, and no doubt "the Secret Chamber in Legree's house," and the "Death of Tom at the Whipping-post," will be faithfully recorded; or, "Legree, the Man of Crime and the Murderer of Uncle Tom," will attract the unwashed inhabitants of the Transpontine districts.

The book, which might have done worlds of good in other hands, will sink into the sewer of literature in penny numbers, and be turned to the worst instead of the best purposes.

The writer here begins with a vague sense of the importance of bringing people "round to our party," presumably the abolitionist cause. By the end of the passage, however, it becomes clear that "our party" implies a like-mindedness of thinking on matters extending beyond American slavery. Indeed, the "worlds of good" which the book might have done echoes *The Times*'s concerns about the political efficacy of Stowe's novel and, more importantly, about the elevating nature of literature, particularly for the working class. In this sense, then, Stowe's novel might have done good had it fallen only into abolitionist hands or had it fallen only into the hands of those readers whose education and common sense (read: "class" and "gender") secured their ability to discern the difference between sterling metal and base fabrications. Having fallen into "other hands," however, such as the "unwashed," who frequent saloons and consume cheap imitations of the more sensational events of the novel, the novel will not do "worlds of good." Lacking the qualities to educate its uncultured readers into the higher realm of interpreting Truth, as *The Times* notes, the novel has not surprisingly ended up in the world of the saloon. It has fallen in with what the letter writer classifies, in a wide sweep of diverse cultural enterprises from saloons to cheap fiction (penny numbers), as the degraded and degrading; it has become what we might today call "low culture." These enterprises cater to the "unwashed," wallowing with them in the "sewer" of their existence. Furthermore, some sense of the impending danger that the existence of a vast number of "the unwashed" poses to the middle class underlines the writer's insistence that this lost opportunity to do "worlds of good" has instead meant doing a world of harm. With *The Times*, then, "A Constant Reader" connects the degeneration of the Victorian reader, of which *Uncle Tom's Cabin* is both a symptom and a cause, with the undermining and dirtying of Victorian society.

This debate about *Uncle Tom's Cabin*, posed in terms of the disposition and quality of the Victorian reader, the function of popular literature, and the effects on Victorian society of improper readers and literature, extended past the coterie of *The Times* and its readers. Beyond that immediate circle, a subsequent review of Stowe's novel in the *Christian Observer* enters the fray as a combatant of *The Times*. The *Christian Observer*'s response to *Uncle Tom's Cabin* grows in part out of an earlier tradition of evangelical suspicion of imaginative literature. The *Christian Observer* was a "patently religious journal" (Sullivan, *British Literary Magazines*, 68) which "attempted to infuse literary criticism with an austere evangelicalism" (73) and viewed the novel as "the most dangerous of all literary forms" (Altick, *The English Common Reader*, 110). But what is important to my discussion here is that the *Christian Observer*'s discussion of *Uncle Tom's Cabin* remains couched precisely within the rhetoric established by *The Times*.

The *Christian Observer*'s review directly sets itself apart from *The Times*: "We feel little sympathy . . . with that strange, capricious, though most powerful Journal, which can discover anything ludicrous or extravagant in the religious faith and spirit of Uncle Tom" (709).[21] The review continues: "We are very far from anticipating those evils under which some newspaper critics, we think, *pretend* to labour, as to the additional violence likely to be awakened by this work in the minds of the slaveholders" (original emphasis, 698). Indeed, unlike *The Times*, the *Christian Observer* insists that violence will be awakened by this text neither in the minds of slaveholders nor in the minds of the readers of England.

This is not to say that the *Christian Observer* is not just as worried as *The Times* about popular literature and its effect on what the review calls "English good sense" (697). Apropos of these concerns, the review begins with a disclaimer of sorts, asserting that: "It is rarely that we call the attention of our readers to works of fiction; both because they are in some degree out of our province, and because we strongly set our faces against the frequent or habitual reading of them" (695). The fault of novels, for the *Christian Observer* as for *The Times*, lies in the way they cultivate the reader's taste:

they excite the feelings, without prompting them to useful action; they create a morbid appetite for what is highly seasoned and stimulating, and so indispose the mind to works of a less exciting but more substantial character; they kindle a sort of blaze of sentimentality, which soon burns out, and leaves, like the fire of the volcano, little behind, but a dark dead mass, useless for any of the purposes of human existence. (695)

Literature, we can extrapolate from this passage, should drive its reader to "useful action" of a "substantial character," enlivening him or her for the cooler "purposes," not the fiery pleasures, "of human existence." As in *The Times*, the *Christian Observer* expresses concern about the existence of a reader susceptible to unhealthy excitement and about the existence of reading matter which will create and feed a "morbid appetite," "indispose the mind," ruin the reader, and likewise ruin the man (or woman).

The review continues by describing "the class of writers" associated with this unhealthy division of literature: popular novels.

The common novelist is a drudge of the meanest description. He is ordinarily well contented to pander to any vulgar or even depraved taste which prevails in the society in which he writes. He watches the gale of public opinion, and trims his vessel accordingly. Is it a profligate age for which he is writing? A licentious tale is immediately provided. Is it an age morbidly craving after excitement? He has ready for the market scenes of horror, mysteries, and murders. Are levity and nonchalance about great and good things the characteristic of the day? He stands forth as the buffoon for the gratification of his readers, and deals out a supply of flippant "badinage," and heartless mockery of good men or great principles. (696)

Notice that "society," "public opinion," and the "market" always already desire the unhealthy, whether it be excitement, licentiousness, or buffoonery. The reader, in this instance, is somehow naturally inclined in the "wrong" direction; the cultivation of his or her taste is a necessary remedy. The popular novelist is an "employe[e] of the public," "its mere echo," content "to pamper the corruptions of the day" (696). But more than that, the popular novelist is the reader's (and society's) "wretched corrupter" (696). To the natural and pre-existing degradation of the reader, the popular novelist contributes his or her additional pollution.

Thus far, the *Christian Observer* covers, if more straightforwardly, much the same territory as *The Times* in its concern over the reader whose natural inclinations are to the kind of popular literature which will contribute to his or her further degradation. Exactly what kind of reader comes under scrutiny in the *Christian Observer* is not clear. He or she may or may not be a member of the newly literate working class to which *The Times* review alludes. What is clear is that the *Christian Observer* shares the concern of *The Times* regarding the potential effects of popular literature on a Victorian reader imagined as uncultured and vulnerable.

Unlike *The Times*, however, the *Christian Observer* "distinguishes" Stowe "from the class of writers [of popular novels] with whom she is not unlikely, at first sight, to be associated" (696). Unlike the corrupt class of popular novelists, Stowe is like "some master-spirit arise[n] to dignify the department which [s]he occupies with higher ends and objects than those proposed to themselves by ordinary artists" (696). The review continues its description of this class of master-spirits to which Stowe belongs:

Far from being the flatterer of the public, he is apt to become its stern and unsparing censor. He warns, cautions, and upbraids. He values his art, not as an end, but as a means. If he aims at popularity, it is for the sake of having weight and influence with his readers; if he is careful to "adorn" his "tale," he will look upon the "painting a moral" as the more essential part of his task. He is in fact merely a modernized edition of the philosopher of the ancient world, catching with proverbs, fables, and parables the attention of those who might be inclined to turn a deaf ear to graver forms of instruction. (697)

The excesses of popularity and financial success of *Uncle Tom's Cabin*, denigrated by *The Times*, are here rewritten as the necessary "means" to a worthy end. The unscrupulous "weapons" which Stowe used to "assail" the "hearts" of her "unsuspecting reader[s]," and which *The Times* excoriated, are for the *Christian Observer* merely the skills of a "master-spirit."

What I want to stress here is that while the *Christian Observer* may differ with *The Times* in its estimate of Stowe's skills, it concurs that the reader's taste is low. Indeed, the *Christian Observer* goes further than *The Times* in suggesting that the reader needs not so much to be developed or cultivated (as *The Times* had recommended) but rather to be manipulated by the "master-spirit." The reader's inclination remains degraded; he or she is still likely "to turn a deaf ear" to more serious and substantial literature. Yet the *Christian Observer* reserves hope that, "under a mark of a witticism," the "master-spirit" may "convey some serious conviction to the mind of the reader" (697).

Like *The Times*'s review, the *Christian Observer*'s ends up being as much about the constitution of the English reader and about what the popular novelist needs to do in order to be successful given the degraded character of his audience as it is about American slavery. *The Times* is anxious about the degradation of the English reader (and of English society), and some of that anxiety spills onto *Uncle Tom's Cabin*. The *Christian Observer*, in contrast, is less concerned with any eventual enlightenment of the reader and, in the meantime, is calm and confident about the ability of the master-spirit to manipulate the vulnerable reader to what *The Times*'s "A Constant Reader" had called "our side." What remains the same in both reviews is the conviction that English readers are prone to degradation, a conviction which overshadows the ostensible subject, *Uncle Tom's Cabin*, in each review.

Earlier, I suggested that the review of *Uncle Tom's Cabin* which appeared in *The Times* articulated the terms of debate on which much further discussion of the text would depend.[22] In closing, I would like to focus on a transformation of the ideological work of *The Times* and the *Christian Observer* in a review of *Uncle Tom's Cabin* in the *Eclectic Review*, a monthly founded on nonconformist principles with a quasi-religious, imperialist tone.[23] The *Eclectic Review* manages to avoid the anxieties about the degraded Victorian (female or working-class) reader of the earlier periodicals by creating a middle-class Victorian subjectivity constructed against the example of an American other.

Like working-class education, English nationalism was a preoccupation for the men and women of mid-Victorian England. In the aftermath of Chartism and the "hungry forties," the 1850s found England in the process of re-constructing itself as a glorious nation prospering in an unprecedented age of Progress: "It was the age of exuberance, of wealth, of invention and audacity . . . It was all part of Progress, and Progress was identical with the spirit of the age" (Ffrench, *The Great Exhibition*, 5). Constructed against other European nations and often more virulently against the example of "Brother Jonathan," the United States, this national identity of "Progress" claimed England's economic, social, political, and moral superiority to the rest of the world.

The issue of slavery was not unrelated to constructions of English superiority; in fact, abolitionism had long served to bolster English nationalism.[24] Slavery was once seen as "a stain on Britain's (mythological/self-promoting) reputation as a freedom-loving land" (original parenthesis, Ferguson, *Subject to Others*, 157), a threat to England's longstanding historical image as a nation where civilization made steady progress, onward and upward. The popular abolitionist campaign of the eighteenth century met that threat and would correlate the emergence of English anti-slavery sentiment with the greatness of the nation. The poet Cowper's famous lines illustrating the Mansfield decision form a case in point of the mobilization of anti-slavery rhetoric for English nationalism. Cowper writes: "Slaves cannot breathe in England; if their lungs / Receive our air, that moment they are free" (qtd. in Ferguson, *Subject to Others*, 187).[25] Like the nation, leading the poor slave out of slavery and leading the rest of the world into a more civilized mode of production, England's air itself is somehow superior. Moreover, it is the quality of *English* air, as much as the fact of slavery or the status of the slave, which is the subject of Cowper's poem.

England, the self-declared leader in the fight for the abolition of the slave trade (1807), would abolish colonial slavery (1833/8) and record its abolition as a national triumph. A passage in the *Anti-Slavery Reporter* illustrates this vision of the history of anti-slavery:

Every one must remember what immense efforts the people of this land had made, in order to abolish slavery in their own dominions; efforts which, under the Divine blessing, were crowned with abundant success . . . nothing was more calculated to delight the philanthropist and the Christian than to witness these results [of abolition], and the unquestionable large amount of blessedness which had ensued.[26]

With the abolition of colonial slavery accomplished and interpreted as a sign of "Divine blessing" upon the English kingdom, English abolitionists turned, in the 1840s and 1850s, to the task of putting their superior Christianity and philanthropy to work by influencing others to abolish slavery. American slavery was the predominant focus of attention; both the heinousness of American slavery and the ongoing relationship of embattled kinship between the United States and England fueled this focus. The same article in the *Anti-Slavery Reporter* records with confidence that "the honest opinion of the people of England, earnestly and faithfully expressed – the honest conviction of the churches of England exercising a legitimate influence on the churches of America – could not fail to produce a powerful effect on America." The "legitimate influence" of English churches and English people on America and American slavery translates into the inevitable power of a superior nation ministering to the wants of a misguided inferior nation.

Within this tradition of the pairing of abolitionism with nationalism, the particular eruption of nationalism on the site of *Uncle Tom's Cabin* in a review in the *Eclectic Review* is both no historical surprise – as is the review in *The Times* with its focus on the nexus between culture and class – and representative of a set of responses to Stowe's novel.[27] If the novel had been forced by *The Times* into a drama about the English reader, it has been forced to operate, in the review in the *Eclectic Review*, in a drama of English nationalism powered by the contemporary ideology of English abolitionism as evidence of England as a superior, freedom-loving land.

Like *The Times*'s review, the *Eclectic Review* also notices the unprecedented popularity of *Uncle Tom's Cabin*, and the reviewer mentions that:

"We have taken some pains to ascertain the extent of its circulation" (720). "Such an effect, so universal and so deep, is a most significant fact," and the reviewer chides *The Times* for belittling such a fact: "It is sheer folly to treat it lightly. The pretence of doing so is mere bravado, the hollowness of which is instantly detected" (720). Whereas *The Times*'s review was anxious about the power of Stowe's novel, especially given its unhealthy influence on the uneducated and uncultured readers of England, the *Eclectic Review* is undisturbed by the success of Stowe's novel. On what basis, then, does the *Eclectic Review* treat the circulation of *Uncle Tom's Cabin* throughout the classes in England with calm, even when the review notes Stowe's comparisons between "the American slave and the English worker" and even when the review complains that Stowe's representation of the condition of the English "labouring people . . . as analogous to those of slavery is [an] outrage [to] common sense" (739)? The answer lies in the review's certainty that the novel's attack on slavery will be understood as an attack on America and American nationalism and as a tribute to the superiority of English abolition and of England generally.

The review begins with a modicum of English humility:

We never recur to the subject of American slavery without pain. It has no attractions for us. Instead of finding pleasure in it we are mortified and abased. As the friends of humanity, we grieve over the wrong done to many of our species; as Englishmen, we are humbled at the part our country has acted in locating slavery in some of the States; and, as Christians, we sorrow in very bitterness of heart at the dishonor done to our holy faith. (717–18)

English mortification at the sight of American slavery and at its own responsibility for helping to create that slavery is swiftly transformed, in this passage, to the larger point: the identification of "Englishmen" as "the friends of humanity," true "Christians," those (only?) who are capable of discerning the purity of "our holy faith" and its pollution through slavery.

The review continues, praising the United States, only to re-assert English superiority:

We rejoice rather that the Anglo-Saxon spirit was sufficiently ripe on the other side of the Atlantic to wrest from the feeble hands of English statesmen a supremacy of which they were unworthy, and which they so little understood. Our feeling towards the American states is that of brotherhood. Attached ourselves to a monarchical government, we cheerfully recognise the many noble features of their republican constitution. We admire their energy, their intelligence, their self-reliance, – nay, we sympathize somewhat with the proud, defiant air with which they stand before the older communities of Europe . . . we are rendered jealous for the good name of America. (718)

An open-minded, sympathetic England looks to its revolutionary brother with pride, this passage seems to suggest, not with bitterness or in ill judgment. But the emphasis, here, is as much on the quality of England, particularly the quality of England's good will for recognizing and being unthreatened by America's difference, as it is on the quality of America.

Further, "exultant hopes" for "the American republic" quickly give way: America has disappointed the world by not being "a new sanctuary, provided in the providence of God, for the freedom which emperors and kings are conspiring to banish from Europe" (718). England, an objectively removed, disinterested observer whose own queen would never conspire with her Parliament to banish freedom, mourns the failure of America to achieve the greatness of a "sanctuary" for freedom.

This same ostensibly disinterested England notices, finally, "the one foul blot which rests on the escutcheon of America" (718): slavery. The "rational" language of the review changes as the review descends into a revelry about American inferiority on this point of slavery:

Call it what they may; palliate its enormity as they please; discourse however fluently on the limits of federal legislation, or fling back passionately on our people, as they are accustomed to do, the charge of originating the system; the thing itself remains – a hideous, misshaped monster. (718)

Slavery is monstrous, and the misguided Americans who belittle the "foul blot" or who try to blame England for its existence reveal instead their own inferiority. Whether or not England originated slavery in America, it is to the national detriment of the United States alone that it remains.

The horrible secrets of their prison house were never before exhibited to so large a multitude, and that too, in a mode calculated to conciliate attention, and so worthy of inspiring confidence. Outraged humanity cries shame on the abettors of such a system, and leaves them no alternative but to abandon its atrocities, or to write themselves outcasts from the virtuous and true-hearted of their race. (738)

The *Eclectic Review*, finally, celebrates *Uncle Tom's Cabin* as a novel of enormous cultural power because it exposes the monstrosity of America and in turn makes clear that the English are superior to all others, particularly the Americans. For the *Eclectic Review*, *Uncle Tom's Cabin* is wonderful because it shows the English to be "the virtuous and true-hearted of their race."

"Uncle Tom" infiltrated England. But England, in turn, appropriated "Uncle Tom," pressing him into the service of contradictory ideological positions. The ubiquity of "Uncle Tom" could conjure the specter of a weak and undiscerning English reader, susceptible to manipulation, who rendered the nation vulnerable, and at the same time serve as a symbol of the philanthropic and moral superiority of England and its people, evoking national unity and strength. "Uncle Tom," like the African-American abolitionist campaign generally, threatened to disturb and disrupt but was also used to re-shape and re-order Victorian identity.

It must be noted that reviews of Stowe's text cannot be taken as unproblematic representations of "Uncle Tom" and his place in Victorian society. The only thing that is clear is that nearly everyone in mid-Victorian England was consuming "Uncle Tom." If we are to believe the *Spectator*'s dismay, Victorians were not consuming "Uncle Tom" in the (ideological) "shapes" preferred by the middle-class periodical press.[28] The attempts above to fix the way in which Stowe's text was read and to control interpretations of *Uncle Tom's Cabin* may serve best as a testament to the middle-class press's inability to harness the transgressive power of "Uncle Tom."

CHAPTER 2

Abolition as a "step to reform in our kingdom": Chartism, "white slaves," and a new "Uncle Tom" in England

England, perhaps more than any other nation, owes a duty to America; and certainly no other people can perform such a duty so effectively as the English. We owe it, then, as a duty to God and to man, and to Americans especially, to speak out against the dreadful oppression of which the black slave is the victim . . . But how shall this voice be expressed? . . . [by] the united declaration of THREE MILLIONS of men, women, and youths of Great Britain against the enslavement of the negro race! *There are three millions of slaves in the United States,– are there not three millions of people in Great Britain who will sign a friendly remonstrance against American slavery? Will not every man assert the right of his fellow-man – every woman the right of her fellow-woman – to freedom?*

(original emphasis and capitalization, *Uncle Tom in England*, 126)[1]

Closing with this exacting injunction that all of England sign and send to America a kind of national petition against slavery, *Uncle Tom in England*, an anonymous[2] novel published in September 1852, two months after *Uncle Tom's Cabin* first appeared in England, is explicitly posed as an amiable companion-piece to Harriet Beecher Stowe's attempt to mobilize the world against American slavery.[3] It is clear that this self-described "Echo, or Sequel" (iii) to *Uncle Tom's Cabin* was conceived to ride the coat-tails of Stowe's extraordinarily popular novel in order to capture its own share of publicity and sales.[4]

And it seemed to succeed at that task. While Forrest Wilson has estimated that *Uncle Tom's Cabin* sold 165,000 copies in England in its first year of circulation (*Crusader*, 419), the precise circulation of *Uncle Tom in England* is more difficult to document. The title page of a subsequent American edition of *Uncle Tom in England* declares this new novel "A Book Selling Equal to 'Uncle Tom's Cabin'" and informs perusers "60,000 Copies Sold – Tenth Edition" (from New York: A. D. Failing edition in the New York Historical Society). Taking into account the fact that such advertisements do not present exact historical evidence, the boasted figure of 60,000 copies suggests a favorable comparison with the numbers for the "ordinary circulating-library novel" which Altick estimates sold in editions of "a thousand or 1,250 copies" and with the figures for cheap editions which Altick estimates sold in "pre-publication printing[s] of 75,000 copies" (*The English Common Reader*, 264, 313).

The circulation and visibility of *Uncle Tom in England* is also confirmed by the number and placement of reviews (not all of high praise). For example, the *Athenaeum*, one of the leading weeklies known for its broad focus on literature, art, and science, notices the novel on October 2, 1852, calling its existence "the inevitable imitation to which [the success of *Uncle Tom's Cabin*] gives birth." The review finds *Uncle Tom in England* "an echo [of *Uncle Tom's Cabin*] of the faintest. The volume, pitch, and quality of the original voice are all lost, – and nothing remains but a travestie of names and characters." The review concludes by marking the writer's "boast" of completing the novel in "seven days and nights" with the following sarcasm: "We should rather he had taken more time – and done better." Another review in the *Spectator* concentrates, perhaps typically for this "liberal, sometimes radical" paper on the anti-Chartist politics of the novel (Sullivan, *British Literary Magazine*, 392): "A sort of sequel to *Uncle Tom*; the freed negro, after sundry adventures, being brought to England; and some hits made at Chartism."

Indeed, as the *Spectator* suggests, *Uncle Tom in England* was designed to do more than just capitalize on the general English interest in American "Uncle Tom." Presenting a newly invented "Uncle Tom" and telling a vastly different story about England's favorite black man, *Uncle Tom in England* seeks to wrest control, authority, and power away from Stowe. Re-shaping his character and his life, *Uncle Tom in England* strives to defuse the transgressive potential of his predecessor's infiltration of Victorian society.

The novel begins on the coast of Africa where two children of Gucongo, an African chief, are being sold with 500 other men, women, and children as war prizes to slavers who will transport the group into American slavery. Renamed Marossi and Rosetta by the slave-ship's captain, the children arrive in Charleston where they are bought by George Harris. Harris, previously known to readers of Stowe's *Uncle Tom's Cabin* as the basically kind but financially embarrassed owner of George and Eliza, is here an "altered man," no longer sympathetic to his slaves; he buys Marossi and Rosetta along with a middle-aged slave named Tom with whom he intends to introduce "a new discipline" (16) to his plantation in Kentucky. On Harris's plantation, this Tom, a different character from Stowe's Tom but also called "Uncle Tom," discovers in another of Harris's slaves his long-lost wife, Susan. Later, their daughter Emmeline, another character from Stowe (the beautiful innocent with whom Cassie escapes from Simon Legree), comes to rescue her long-lost parents with the aid of a kind Quaker family, the Hanaways. Marossi, Rosetta, and Susan escape to the Hanaways, but Tom is caught at the last minute.

Tom is tried and sentenced to death for helping other slaves to escape; Emmeline, meanwhile, dies of grief and worry. A great outcry is raised, particularly from England, over Tom's trial and sentence; as a result, Tom goes unpunished and is bought out of slavery. Tom, Susan, Marossi, and Rosetta now go to England, both to escape any danger and to work to influence public opinion against American slavery. In England, Tom and Susan meet Chartists and discuss the shared plights of "white slaves and black slaves" (116). They decide that "we must make common cause and help each other!" (120): the black American slave and the white English worker must join forces in peaceful attempts to promote change. Thomas, the Hanaways' son, marries Rosetta. The two move to Canada and are praised by the Quaker Hanaways since "every such act of amalgamation contributes to break down the prejudice of the separate races" (123). Marossi goes to Africa as a missionary.

Uncle Tom in England is stocked with the conventions of writing about slavery: scenes of slave life, the thrill of escape, and all the standard discussions of the injustices of the slave system. Yet the tropes common to literature about slavery are displaced in this novel by an overwhelming emphasis on social position. In effect, the novel translates the issues of American slavery into the home-grown English discourse of class.[5]

In its initial pages, for example, the narrative focuses on how the African-born children, Rosetta and Marossi, are inherently superior to those around them. The narrative describes the ways in which they differentiate themselves both from the other slaves aboard the slave-ship and from the rough and unmannered black and white working-class crew who man the ship. The children are distinguished physically as "likely little ones [who] will fetch well in the market . . . being pretty, and sleek" (8–9); moreover, their emotional bond, "always holding each other's hands, and often embracing lovingly, and whispering words which none understood but themselves" (11), reveals them as highly developed moral creatures. The children's beauty and domestic virtue are matched by a seemingly inherent sense of social position: Rosetta and Marossi segregate themselves from the other slaves and gravitate instead towards the sailors, in particular, the Captain, whose social standing is marked both by his rank and by the standardized diction of his speech (in contrast to the dialect of the mates). All of this is underlined by the facts of Rosetta's and Marossi's birth: as the children of an African chief, they represent not ordinary Africans but an aristocracy among the savages.

In this sense, the children resemble the transplanted orphans who populate so many Victorian novels: their physical appearance, behavior, and internal virtue render visible a class status obscured by their unfortunate circumstances.[6] Moreover, the reader is assured that this kind of social dislocation will not remain uncorrected, that the young hero and heroine will be restored to the social position from which they were unjustly ousted. The conventional happy ending the children achieve re-assures Victorians that the social order really outweighs unlucky circumstances, even such horrendous circumstances as slavery. Like the dispossession of Oliver Twist, cast into a lower station to which he did not belong, the oppression of Rosetta and Marossi is vilified. The novel insists (and I use the racially coded cliché deliberately) that cream will rise to the top; those who, like Rosetta and Marossi, ought not to be slaves will escape.

Because the novel stresses Rosetta and Marossi's exceptionalness, its protest against slavery is muffled. Like many abolitionist texts, *Uncle Tom in England* registers a fundamental ambivalence about the need for a larger social overhaul in which all black men and women, deserving or not, would be freed from slavery.[7] The novel avoids the question of whether human worth is constituted by race or skin color,[8] but it insists that social class is natural, that one's place in the world is always determined by and will eventually correspond with one's physical and moral value. What this means, as we will see below, is that the novel concedes that some men and women (black and white) are inferior and their inherent inferiority justifies the degraded circumstances of their lives.[9]

If the exceptional Rosetta and Marossi do not deserve the violent upheaval and displacement of the slave trade and slavery, the future for Tom and Susan is far less secure. Lacking the good birth and innate superiority that ensure Rosetta's and Marossi's success, Tom and Susan struggle to attain what Rosetta and Marossi seem "naturally" to possess. Their fight to lift themselves up and thus to earn the privilege of freedom bears the strong imprint of the middle-class Victorian discourse of working-class self-improvement.

The key to this discourse is education. For the middle class in mid-Victorian England, according to Dorothy Thompson, the thinking on this subject went as follows: "anyone who is not educated is not anything. Literacy is the test of humanity" (*The Chartists*, 241). The working class, by and large uneducated, at least by the standards of the middle class, were in this sense less than human. By mid-century, however, there was an explosion of working-class education. The attempts of working men and women to acquire proof of humanity, however,[10] were met with a concomitant anxiety, on the part of the middle class, about the consequences of education for these new groups of people. In the same way as they were preoccupied with measuring and maintaining the taste and character of the newly-educated readers entering the emerging literary marketplace discussed in the last chapter, the middle class were obsessed with the idea that the working class would now have access to that which had once served as a "trump card in . . . class competition" (Best, *Mid-Victorian Britain*, 150). Anxieties about working-class education were mollified through a variety of philanthropic undertakings. Foremost among these was "provided" education which could be touted to the working class as the medium for class improvement and social mobility but safely underwritten by the unstated goal of trying "to raise a new race of working people – respectful, cheerful, hard-working, loyal, pacific, and religious" (Johnson, "Educational Policy," 119). Education, in other words, was fundamentally about social control of the working class.

Of course, "knowledge is power" is also a common and important trope in the genre of slave narratives. The acquisition of knowledge, particularly literacy, is often represented in the slave narrative as a scene of figurative emancipation and psychological empowerment after which the journey towards physical emancipation begins.[11] For example, Frederick Douglass in his *Narrative of the Life of Frederick Douglass* (1845) discusses how a kind mistress begins to teach him to read and write. "Mistress," Douglass writes, "in teaching me the alphabet, had given me the *inch*, and no precaution could prevent me from taking the *ell*" (original emphasis, 53). Douglass directly links the acquisition of literacy skills with his burgeoning desire for freedom. He writes:

the thought of being *a slave for life* began to bear heavily upon my heart. Just about this time, I got hold of a book entitled "The Columbian Orator." Every opportunity I got, I used to read this book. Among much of other interesting matter, I found in it a dialogue between a master and his slave . . . In this dialogue, the whole argument in [*sic*] behalf of slavery was brought forward by the master, all of which was disposed of by the slave. The slave was made to say some very smart as well as impressive things in reply to his master – things which had the desired though unexpected effect; for the conversation resulted in the voluntary emancipation of the slave on the part of the master. (original emphasis, 54)

This particular reading material and his education generally help Douglass to articulate his discontent, and this articulation, in turn, initiates the start of his actual journey towards freedom.

Susan's and Tom's struggle for education engages both these discourses. As in Douglass's experience, Susan's education is thoroughly intertwined with her struggle for freedom and her reading materials contain both figuratively and literally the keys to that freedom. For example, Susan says that she "looked for encouragement to the examples of Pennington, Douglass, Cuffe [*sic*], Garnet, Bayley,[12] and others of whom she had heard and read, and she resolved that she would succeed, in the struggle [for freedom], or die in the attempt." Her study also includes the "Life of Washington" which contains "a map of the United States [and] knowledge of the country through which she must pass, and the distance she would have to travel" (41). With "examples" and "encouragement," metaphorical maps of her personal journey, as well as maps of the physical landscape, Susan's education sets her free.

Tom also experiences empowerment through education:

Under Susan's influence, Tom's heart became enlarged, and his mind developed. He was no longer a slave, though in fetters . . . It is astonishing how rapidly truth takes root, when its seeds are cast upon a soil rich with the elements of productiveness, yet long left neglected and uncultivated. Every new truth which entered Tom's mind . . . produced a rich harvest for the struggle in which Tom subsequently engaged. His very words, in course of time, became refined, his manners less harsh and mechanical. (40–1)

Tom's education, detailed as "Susan's influence" and as a "harvest" of the mind, figuratively and psychologically frees him from slavery and prefigures the literal freedom Tom will shortly attain.

Acquiring education, Tom and Susan can reap their reward. Education is the key not just to the salvation of the soul but to literal mobility. Susan and Tom escape from slavery to live happily in England where, the novel tells us, "Uncle Tom and Susan fulfilled a sphere of immense usefulness in the advocacy of the abolition of slavery" (123). Now "useful" workers in the dignified fight against slavery, Tom and Susan have made it.

It is important to notice how the exploration of the power of education for the slave is underwritten here by the ideology of "provided" education. Education is not just about finding one's way out of the psychological and physical prison of slavery; it is about the re-making of the self.

Two examples betray the middle-class educational agenda undergirding the narrative of education within the novel. Returning to Susan's course of study, we see that her reading influences not just her ability to escape but her very identity. She tells Tom: "I have 'The Life of Franklin,' 'The Life of Washington,' a part of Milton's works, some of 'Shakspere's [sic], the 'Life of William Penn,' the 'Life of Howard,' the 'Life of Gustavus Vasa Equiano,' the 'Narratives' of 'Pennington,' of 'Douglass,' and of 'Phillis Wheatley.'"[13] This literature has, Susan says, "Taught me to know myself." Knowing herself, Susan's "mission," as she terms it, is to teach Tom "to speak well and correctly," to transform Tom through the process of education so that he too may "know" himself. That Susan names Tom's course of study a "mission" underscores that this is not a vision of education in which knowledge facilitates the emergence of some inner self; Tom is imagined here as a savage for whom education will be not revealing but transforming (30).

The second example which illustrates the political agenda underlying the educational program of the novel occurs near the start of the story, at the moment when Tom and Susan are first reunited: "Tom perceived, in the course of this conversation, that during his separation from his wife, a great deal of refinement had been acquired by her; she had become, in fact, the greatest lady he ever knew, and had picked up such a lot of learning that he could scarcely understand her at times" (27). Education is here most explicitly revealed as "refinement." Susan's transformation is ultimately defined neither by her self-knowledge nor by her quest for freedom but by the appellation Tom uses: Susan had become a "lady." Ironically the source of less, not more, communication between husband and wife, Susan's evolution is tellingly registered in the language of social class.

Uncle Tom in England thus follows the pattern of most writing about slavery. Many of these works, including slave narratives authored by African-Americans, struggle to wage their protests against the harsh conditions of slavery while at the same time working to make themselves accessible and comprehensible to readers by operating within the literary and social conventions of the historical moment – in this case, conventions about the relationship between self-worth and social position. Interestingly, *Uncle Tom in England* eschews the traditional economy of literature about slavery in which skin color correlates with self-worth and social position; this novel maps its characters along a seemingly color-blind scale. The scale remains, however, and, for Victorians, its calibrations – birth, virtue, and education – were politically weighty.

Uncle Tom in England's politics cannot be explained, however, as the simple correlative of literary or social conventions. For the novel pursues more than just a hackneyed English translation and transposition of American slavery. Capitalizing on the popularity of slavery as a literary theme, writing from the moral high ground of the anti-slavery movement, and manipulating the powerful rhetoric of abolition, the novel engages in a deliberate act of cultural appropriation.

I suggested earlier that the fight by Tom and Susan to lift themselves up from the lowly station of slavery bears the imprint of the middle-class Victorian discourse of working-class self-improvement. In fact, Tom and Susan are explicitly identified with the English white working class; their unifying bond is ignorance. Susan tells Tom that when Milton wrote, "knowledge was not so diffused as now, and there were people in England who knew as little of truth, as our unfortunate race now does" (46). She continues, explaining that black American slaves are like this distant English working class: "we are in the same position as those ignorant people, from whom the rulers of the olden time would have excluded the light" (46). Ironically, while this passage works to consider the relation between the oppressions of class and slavery, the novel here turns from current realities, as if working-class exclusion was a thing of history and as if "knowledge" and "truth" were fully diffused in nineteenth-century England. With the issue of English class oppression firmly re-assigned to the distant past, the novel is stripped of any progressive potential.

Obviously, all such oppression in England was not far distant. Thomas Carlyle was one of the many Victorian thinkers to consider this issue and in "Signs of the Times" he identifies ignorance of what *Uncle Tom in England* terms "the light" as one of the consequences of the Industrial Age: "By our skill in Mechanism, it has come to pass, that in the management of external things we excel all other ages; while in whatever respects the pure moral nature, in true dignity of soul and character, we are perhaps inferior to most civilized ages" (*Selected Works*, 35). Without explicitly singling out the working class as the ones with the problem of "moral" inferiority of "soul and character," Carlyle offers a solution of reform that threatens no one. Describing the scope of his task as "To reform a world," Carlyle writes that "to reform a nation, no wise man will undertake; and all but foolish men know, that the only solid, though far slower reformation, is what each begins and perfects on *himself*" (original emphasis, 44). A radical reorganization of the Victorian world, in other words, would be unwise. Carlyle envisions the world re-made by the self-perfection of the English worker; like Susan's "mission" to overcome the "defect" of the slave, Carlyle's plan encompasses self-improvement but not social reform.

We have seen already how *Uncle Tom in England* applies this Carlylean program of "slower reformation" (44) to the problem of American slavery – freeing the deserving and placing the burden of earning freedom on those slaves who are not exceptional in their birth or breeding. The second half of the novel turns directly to the issue of working-class reform, insisting that this too can be achieved through a peaceful, orderly movement based on the idea of individual transformation. In this pursuit, *Uncle Tom in England* proceeds as if the transformations of worker and slave were strictly parallel, as if both needed only education to begin the self-improvement that leads to freedom, and as if the Chartist and abolitionist movements were articulated around projects of individual self-improvement rather than more radical collective change.

The novel initiates its focus on the problems of the English working class by producing a distorted rewriting of Chartism, resuscitating the virtually defunct working-class reform movement as a nearly unrecognizable Carlylean movement aimed only at slow, individual "reformation." In the world of the novel, Chartists can be divided into two distinct categories: those who advocate physical force versus those who advocate moral force. This division does not reflect the historical reality of the movement in which "no clear line of demarcation [existed] between the two types of method or between the men who inclined to the one or the other." In fact, while moral-force Chartists believed that "they could carry the Charter by means of public meetings, agitation, petitions and direct or indirect influence at the polls," physical force Chartists differed only in their sense that these measures might not prove sufficient and that "sooner or later an armed insurrection would be necessary [and acceptable] to force the government to yield" (Slosson, *The Decline of the Chartist Movement*, 83).[14] Viewed through the novel's distorting lens, however, physical-force Chartism represents the danger of violent anarchy through the irresponsible actions of unenlightened men, whereas moral-force Chartism articulates middle-class values such as the self-education and self-improvement of the working man.[15] These representations are personified in two characters: William Clarke, a moral-force Chartist, who stands opposed and superior, not just politically but morally, to Richard ("Dick") Boreas, a physical-force Chartist.

Dick complains that he has not had any work and that he and his family are starving. He argues that this misery justifies his, and by extension any, unlawful actions against the government:

Ain't I justified in fighting? –ain't I justified in stealing? –ain't I justified in doing anything to get food and clothing for myself and those who look to me for help? What matters it to me if the hinstitutions of the country, as they calls 'em, fall to pieces? We can't live upon hinstitutions, and constitutions, and them d—d things; it's our rights as we wants – it's the Charter – to let us manage our own affairs, and not let 'em tax us and grind us in the way they do. (114)

Violence, according to Dick, is morally acceptable when the institutions of society, such as Parliament, have become so grossly unjust that they "grind" the people.[16]

The odds, however, are stacked against Dick and the philosophies of physical-force Chartism. Described as an "idle," "drunken man" who might work more if he applied himself but who instead indulges his vices and beats his wife (115), Dick is thoroughly discredited by the novel.[17] Moreover in the passage above, Dick's ideas are trivialized by his flawed mispronunciation; his misnaming of "hinstitutions" stands as a signal of his general ignorance of and inability to understand or critique institutions. Because of the presentation of Dick as one of the unenlightened, his indictments of English institutions as corrupt bureaucratic machines can be easily dismissed by the novel.

Not content with belittling Dick and depicting the representatives of physical-force Chartism as men who lack good "habits and opinions" and "cannot govern [themselves]" (115) let alone the nation, the novel ensures the repudiation of physical-force Chartism by associating it with the bogeyman of Victorian England – the French Revolution.[18]

[W]hat have violent revolutions ever done? . . . What have they done in France – do they enjoy liberty there? No. And you will find that in proportion to the revolutions by force, which occur in any country, so do the liberties of the people decline. These fighting Chartists destroy our chances of success. They are, as a body, people defective of habits and opinions. (115)

Should physical-force Chartism ever succeed by violent revolution in actually toppling the institutions of society and giving power to these masses of unelevated, unenlightened people, the result, the novel insists, would be disaster.

It is worth noting that, even within the context of the fight against slavery, Dick Boreas's argument that oppression justifies violence would have been worrisome to middle-class Victorians. *The Times*, for example, while it recognizes the "stain" of slavery, warns that violence in the name of abolition may produce Arnoldian "anarchy and confusion" (*Culture and Anarchy*, 97): "Hate begets hate, and a war of races secures the rapid deterioration and decline of all the combatants. We may well shrink before rashly inviting so bloody and disastrous a conflict" ("Uncle Tom's Cabin").[19] The non-violent escape of a few deserving individuals, such as Tom, Susan, and the children, is acceptable; more radical, large-scale social upheaval portends, for *The Times*, an undesirable "war of races."

Reactions to the bloody insurrection of John Brown at Harper's Ferry (1859) demonstrate the same antipathy towards the use of violence. "[T]here was no use disguising the fact that he was prepared to defend himself, even to blood, if any attempt were made to prevent the success of his enterprise," concedes the *Anti-Slavery Reporter*. The paper cannot expect such an enterprise to be acceptable to Victorians and thus it works to re-construct Brown's use of violence as a defense against, rather than an initiation of, violence.

John Brown went not as an insurgent against peaceable men, but against an armed band of insurgents. Blood was there already – blood, drop by drop wrung from the hearts of poor defenseless people, deprived of every means of freedom. He interfered; he saw a strong man in the act of beating out the brains of a weak man, and he interposed himself between.

The sanction of Brown's use of violence to overthrow the institution of slavery is won by the fact that violence preceded Brown, that armed conflict was already in place in the United States. Thus, Brown was not commencing "mad" anarchy but merely reacting to it. It is the slaveholders, "an armed band of insurgents," who are portrayed as the rash and the violent. Further, the *Anti-Slavery Reporter* characterizes Brown's endeavor not as social upheaval, not as the overthrow of the institution of slavery, but as an attempt to obtain for a few "poor defenseless people" the chance of freedom, an attempt to help "a weak man" who is being unjustly beaten by "a strong man." Only by downplaying Brown's attacks on the institution of slavery and by constructing Brown's attack as an attempt to restore peace and order can the *Anti-Slavery Reporter* condone his violent insurrection.

Turning, then, from the drunken, uneducated, and irresponsible advocates of physical-force Chartism and the violence about which Victorians were so skittish, the novel presents William Clarke, representative of the model working class and of (morally superior) moral-force Chartism. Unlike the unemployed Dick Boreas, Clarke is introduced to the reader as "an intelligent mechanic" (115).[20] Gone is the parodic language of the people; Clarke speaks in formal, rational language. And while Richard Boreas owns the nickname "Dick"[21] and the unusual, unflattering "Boreas"[22] (with its connotations that Dick is a bore and an ass), William Clarke remains respectfully addressed as "William."

With physical-force Chartism dismissed, the novel uses its endorsement of Clarke to present a reform agenda which poses no threat to the social and political status quo. Clarke begins by suggesting that he shares Boreas's sense that England's institutions are to blame for the social discontent among the lower classes. All similarity between Clarke's and Boreas's political positions, however, ends there. Clarke argues that these institutions are necessary and benevolent, if temporarily malfunctioning. He explains to Tom and Susan that "much of this evil [both the inadequate social conditions of working-class life and the violence they provoke in physical-force Chartists] arises not so much from political as from social misgovernment." English "good institutions" have become "enfeebled," and Clarke proposes that "an enlightened system of education . . . would suffice to enlighten the minds of the whole of these degraded creatures, or as many of them as are capable of, or willing to receive it" (116). Finally, for Clarke, it is not so much that the institutions of society are to blame for the existing social problems, but that the working classes have never been properly "enlightened." Clarke sounds a Carlylean note in his insistence that the solution lies in self-improvement: the working class needs to "acquire the power of governing themselves" (115). Just as Tom's literal freedom was a nearly automatic consequence of his education ("He was no longer a slave, though in fetters" [40]), the novel suggests, by way of Clarke, that following enlightenment the "gates of liberty will fly open of their own accord" for the working classes.

It is important to notice that Clarke's argument labels the working class as not only "degraded" but responsible for their own degradation and concedes that education will "enlighten" and "relieve" only some of the working class: "as many of them as are capable of, or willing to receive it" (116). Recall that the novel's protest against slavery was launched only for those black slaves who, because of birth and virtue or self-improvement, had shown themselves worthy of freedom. In both cases, the novel insists that only those who lift themselves up (together of course with those who are born enlightened) deserve freedom from oppression. In the end, pitting physical-force Chartism, constructed as violently and politically irresponsible, against moral-force Chartism, constructed as rational and peaceable, the novel secures support only for reform made, as Matthew Arnold put it, "by due course of law" (97).

Why does the novel pick a fight with physical-force Chartism when the entire Chartism movement, by the time of the publication of this novel in 1852, is, if not dead, then on its last legs?[23] And why, in revivifying Chartism, does the author give character to physical- and moral-force Chartism, so as to replay a contest between the two that is, by 1852, moot? The answer, I believe, is that the novel, like many of the industrial novels written after the demise of Chartism, wants to celebrate and glorify England: in particular, England's management of its own reform movements.[24] In the face of the 1848 revolutions in Europe and with what the English perceived as the time bomb of slavery steadily ticking away in the United States, a revisionist depiction of Chartism, caricatured and hamstrung as the movement is by the novel, serves to authorize for the English a nostalgic pride over the nation's superior handling of its domestic reform problems and a sense of international superiority.[25]

Depicting moral-force Chartism as a movement for self-improvement, as a movement basically at peace with the existing structure of society, and discrediting physical-force Chartism as the irrational whim of drunken uneducated men, *Uncle Tom in England*'s re-writing of the history of the movement allows the novel to suggest that Chartism, at least all of Chartism that ever really made any sense, succeeded. The novel can claim that Chartism's real goals, self-enlightenment and self-education, have been peacefully achieved and incorporated into mainstream Victorian society. (This explains why Clarke is never allowed to speak specifically about universal male suffrage, the crucial goal of all Chartists, which was incontrovertibly not achieved.) Moreover, the defeat and disappearance of physical-force Chartism is justified by its depiction as a misguided upstart movement doomed by its internal anarchy and confusion and by the incompetence of its members. *Uncle Tom in England*, then, refutes any suggestion that the Chartist movement was squelched by those in power and paints a picture of England as a leader among nations, gracefully accommodating social change and promoting justice.[26]

What should be clear by this point is that the abolition of slavery is not the ultimate agenda of *Uncle Tom in England*. An examination of the novel's argumentative, clumsy, and deliberately paradoxical subtitle, "A Proof that Black's White," confirms this. One might conjecture that the awkwardness of the subtitle stems from the fact that the novel's ostensible purpose – to prove black is white – goes against the grain of Victorian common sense. Despite the popularity of the "Am I Not a Man and a Brother?" abolitionist slogan, few among nineteenth-century Victorians would have accepted the idea that blacks could or should be the political, social, cultural, or moral equals of whites.[27] Furthermore, the publication of the novel in 1852 places it within a period during which attitudes about race and ethnicity in England were undergoing a reconfiguration which would culminate in the imperialism of the turn of the century.[28]

The novel offers an explanation for its seemingly provocative subtitle:

The intention of this work has been to show, in the words of its title, "that Black's White." By this is meant that there is no natural disqualification of the black population, which should deprive them of the right to enjoy equal political and social privileges with ourselves; or, in the words of Uncle Tom, in his defence, it has been attempted to prove that "as far as our colored brethren have had the advantages of education and of civilization, they have been as peaceful, as orderly, as devout, as those of fairer skin." (123)

The phrase "no natural disqualification" effectively sidesteps the issue of racial equality. While "education" and "civilization" may produce "colored brethren" who are as "peaceful," "orderly," and "devout" as whites, the passage's back-handed string of negatives – "*no* natural *dis*qualification of the black population, which should *deprive* them of the right" (my emphasis) – stops short of demanding political and social privileges for blacks.

More importantly, the passage speaks of "qualifications." If "there is no *natural* disqualification of the black population" (my emphasis), there are still those who are disqualified. The exceptionally qualified (like Rosetta and Marossi) or those who earn their qualifications through "education" and "civilization" (like Tom and Susan) may win privileges. Those without the necessary qualifications, however, such as Dick Boreas or the slaves whom Tom and Susan left behind on George Harris's farm, may be justly deprived. In other words, the unstated connection between black and white in the contraction "black's white" seems to be that the white working class are no more "naturally" qualified for the political and social privileges of society than are black slaves. Both the white working class and the black slaves, the novel implies, may be disqualified and denied privileges.

If the novel's title provides a strange and slightly obscure argument for the color-blind deprivation of both black slaves and white workers, an equally unexpected argument is suggested, near the end of the novel, for the interdependence of Chartism and abolitionism. William Clarke argues not only that the campaign to abolish American slavery is connected to rather than in competition with Chartism, but that abolition must take precedence over Chartism.[29] He says:

> We have . . . our grievances. Where is the country that has not? But this I believe, – that we have more real liberty in England than is enjoyed in any other kingdom in the world. But we can't make much advance while what are called the enlightened governments maintain such oppressions as they do. What do our opponents tell us here? "Why," say they, "look to America; there they have your vaunted charter, and there are three million of slaves bowed to the very dust." I consider, therefore, that a very important step to reform in our kingdom would be the abolition of slavery by the republic of America. (115)

Clarke's reasoning, in other words, is that abolition is a stage in the fight for Chartism. And he bases his prioritizing of the two reform agendas not on some sense that the cause of the "white slave" and the cause of the black slave are linked but on the idea of the responsibilities of "enlightened governments."

Under this rubric of national chauvinism comes a moral and political charge: England and America set the standards of reform and lead the rest of the world in the right direction. In general, the novel insists that "Reciprocal influences prevail between nations as among individuals – and one nation may determine the conduct of another nation as effectually as one man may exercise suasion upon the mind of his fellow." England, for example, having kindled the "flame" of the Anti-Corn Law-League "lights up a kindred element in European nations . . . [t]he eyes of Europe have been upon England during the recent struggle, and her example has extended its influence wherever misgovernment exists" (125).

On the other hand, the United States, having lit the "flame" of English Chartism with its "vaunted" American charter, has failed to shine its beacon of light onto England because the stain of slavery blocks that light. England might "look to America," to America's accomplishment of the charter, but the accomplishment can only be seen in the context of the "three million of slaves bowed to the very dust." Despite the so-called advance of the charter, America still permits slavery. Since even without a charter England claims "more real liberty" than anywhere else, England does not look up to the American charter for guidance, it looks down on that charter, scorning the "American constitution [as] the greatest anomaly in the world" (120).

America has failed to enlighten the world, and England is among "the nations throughout the world" for whom American slavery is proving a "stumbling block" (123). This is why Clarke prioritizes the fight against American slavery. With the stumbling block of the contradiction of the existence of slavery in a nation which has a charter, England cannot achieve Chartist reform.

The proposition that American reform must be primary, that the contradiction of America's lack of freedom hinders English reform, however, suggests that influence in the "kinship" of "enlightened governments" flows from the United States to England. In the example of the Anti-Corn-Law League, influences flow in one direction: from England to the rest of Europe. With the abolition of slavery, influences also flow from England: having abolished colonial slavery, England sends its influence on such matters to the United States which takes the lesson from its superior and goes to work on the reform. Indeed, the novel, originally published in England but subsequently circulated in America as a piece of anti-slavery advocacy, offers itself as an example of just such an influence, a literary beacon sent with moral and political purpose from the enlightened nation of England to America.

But are we really to believe that England, this center of influence, cannot accomplish Chartist reform without the influence of American reform? Why would England look to America at all, let alone allow the instance of the failed charter in America to stand in the way of reform in England? Are we to believe that in this instance (alone) England looks to the influence and leadership of the United States, using the American charter to set an example for English Chartism?

The reversal of the transatlantic power relations is convenient for undermining the urgency of Chartist reforms, but it is ultimately unconvincing. For all the while the United States is accorded this particular role of leadership in the instance of American slavery, the novel firmly insists that England is the *real* leader among nations. The critique of the American Constitution as a "vaunted charter" is a critique of American nationalism and an attempt to reaffirm English superiority. It forms part of a series of taunts running through the novel focused specifically on the icons of American nationalism, particularly the American flag, in which English nationalism is constructed and affirmed against the model of the United States. For example, when the slave-ship carrying Marossi and Rosetta arrives in the United States, "in the harbor of Charleston," the novel plays on the ironic juxtaposition of symbols: "the American flag of stars and stripes floating at its mainmast!" (11). This joust resonates with the many sarcastic references to the stars and stripes of the American flag throughout the abolitionist campaign: the "national flag was the symbol of their [both the slaves' and the Americans'] shame; the white man might aspire to the stars, while for the poor black man there was no reward but stripes" (Wright, *An Historical Parallel*, 2–3).[30] Entitled "The Stripes and Stars of America," the chapter which describes Tom's trial continues this jab, illustrating his protest against the injustice of a legal system which would condemn him for seeking his and his family's freedom as a scene of "vaunted," specious American justice.

A number of other passages work as both obloquies to the United States and accolades to England. For example, during the auction at which Tom is sold to George Harris, the auctioneer announces that Tom is a Christian. The novel queries sarcastically, "What think you, Christian reader, would the repetition of this qualification have enhanced the value of the lot? 'Going – a *Christian* – for four hundred dollars!' Who, on *this* side of the Atlantic, will bid another fifty?" (original emphasis, 16). While Americans bid for and barter in human flesh, the novel confidently asserts the difference across the Atlantic. No English citizen, the passage presumes, would add fifty to the count.

Debunking America's advances (the charter) and symbols of advancement (the American flag), since none represent real progress in the achievement of liberty, the Englishman or woman can feel superior to his or her American counterpart. Likewise, the novel asserts, the Englishman need not feel any national inferiority based on the comparatively large size of the United States:

The Yankee . . . looks upon this little island . . . and taunts us with wanting elbow room. There is one thing, we confess, we cannot find room for here, and that is slavery – traffic in human bodies to the sacrifice of human souls. And from our hearts we deplore the humiliating fact that so vast a country as

America – a country boasting of free institutions, and having a constitution in which the rights of mankind are nobly asserted, should be stained by so foul a spot, her name a byeword [*sic*] among nations, a reproach upon the tongues of honest men! (17)

Rather than representing its superiority to England, the size of the United States and its relative advances in freedom, such as the Bill of Rights and the Constitution, come to represent instead the meagerness of the United States. Little England, with its ancient monarchic institutions, without the benefit of grand size and the grand institutions of freedom, is made to look that much the better in contrast.

Such explicit praises of England recur throughout the novel. England "has already heard and heeded the voice of slaves, and struck off their shackles!" (94); the fact that England eliminated the slave trade and colonial slavery is a commonly cited source of national pride. Tom praises England as "a truly Christian land [with] a peculiarly Christian people" (110). England is even represented as a land free of color prejudice. As Susan tells Tom, "Phillis Wheatley was a poor negress . . . she went to England, a beautiful country, where there are people of great minds and noble hearts, and where men and women are not bought and sold, and there she was treated as a child of God without reference to the color of her skin" (30). Likewise, we see the entire family treated with kindness and respect in England, conversing with rich and poor without remark upon their complexions.

In all of these comparisons between England and a belittled United States, we see England constructing itself as the true leader among nations.[31] Ironically, the very examples the novel uses expose the contradictions within this tidy national façade. The novel's self-congratulation that in England, "we cannot find room for . . . slavery – traffic in human bodies to the sacrifice of human souls" (127) flies in the face of several decades of criticism of the treatment of women and child laborers and of the working class generally. Indeed, it flies in the face of criticism that established "white slavery" as the name for that treatment; by 1850, the "slavery of the working class" had become the dominant term around which the plight of the condition of the working class was debated.[32] Elsewhere, when insisting that "there is no natural disqualification of the black population, which should deprive them of the right to enjoy equal political and social privileges with ourselves" (123), the novel placidly creates an England, "ourselves," in which all enjoy political and social privileges, an England which bears little resemblance to reality.[33]

Contradictions notwithstanding, then, the novel politically contorts itself in order to construct this vision of a superior England set against the example of a besieged America.[34]

Appropriating the slave's story and exploiting its popularity, *Uncle Tom in England* attempts to redress and harness the transgressive power of "Uncle Tom." Victorian readers can still enjoy the pleasures of the company of "Uncle Tom," but they will read of his troubles and his travails in a novel which also serves as a kind of national autobiography, confirming for middle- and upper-class Victorians English national superiority and the security of the nation's cherished values: stability, order, and slow progress. First, the novel assures its readers that the values they hold dear are just: internal value, measured in terms of birth and virtue, always corresponds with social status; those who are deserving in life will always be rewarded. Second, it seeks to persuade those readers that these values actually underpin Chartism and abolitionism: abolitionism and Chartism are reform movements structured by the ethic of self-improvement, not a vision of widespread social transformation, movements which can be celebrated as posing no threat to the social and political status quo. Thus *Uncle Tom in England* allows its readers to revel in their support of a hamstrung version of American abolitionism while at the same time assuaging any anxieties about England's treatment of Chartism and its own "white" slaves.[35]

In blunt terms, *Uncle Tom in England* stages a literary version of a cultural trafficking in black bodies and black experiences to produce a powerful narrative of English national superiority for the English middle class.[36] Ironically, "Uncle Tom" had experienced this treatment already; Harriet Beecher Stowe had "adapted" Josiah Henson's story to fit her purposes in *Uncle Tom's Cabin*.[37] But African-Americans would be travelling in England over the next decade: speaking, writing, appearing on platforms, telling their own stories. Victorians concerned about their nation's consumption of American abolitionism and of the consequences of such consumption would find that re-inventing and re-writing these flesh-and-blood men and women posed different challenges than had the fictional "Uncle Tom."

CHAPTER 3

"Repetitious accounts so piteous and so harrowing":
the ideological work of American slave narratives in England

"Uncle Tomism has had its day," reports an 1853 essay in the *Westminster Review*, but "Slave tales continue to be the literary staple among the products of the American press [exported to England]. The ladies of England are so interested in 'those dear blacks'" ("American Slavery and Emancipation," 298). Whether or not *Uncle Tom's Cabin* had met its demise by 1853, tales of slavery were indeed a "staple" in the Victorian literary marketplace: at least twenty American slave narratives appeared in English editions[1] by mid-century, and it is likely that other narratives circulated in American editions. The catalogues of Mudie's Select Library, that institution of Victorian society and "the surest guide to the make-up of the mid Victorian public and what it read" (Terry, *Victorian Popular Fiction*, 6), list the narratives of Frederick Douglass (1845) and Solomon Northup (1853) among the offerings available to subscribers.[2] Slave narratives, R. J. M. Blackett writes,

sold faster than they could be printed. Pennington's quickly sold six thousand copies and ran through three editions between August, 1849, and July, 1850. William Wells Brown's went through three British, two American, one French, and one German edition. In 1844, Roper estimated that he had sold twenty-five thousand copies of the English edition that first appeared in 1837 . . . by 1856 the English edition had gone through ten printings . . . Those who could not afford to buy their own copies borrowed them from others, and they were read in churches, Sunday schools, mechanics institutes, and working-class associations. (*Building an Antislavery Wall*, 25–6)

C. Peter Ripley concurs with Blackett's findings and adds that in England the narratives sold "well, probably better than in America, as a rule" (*The Black Abolitionist Papers*, 20).

My thanks to audiences at the Center for Critical Analysis of Contemporary Culture, Rutgers University; at the Tampa, FL, meeting of the Research Society for Victorian Periodicals; and at the conference, "The Victorians and Race," University of Leicester, for their comments on and interest in this work. I also want to acknowledge Lisa Botshon, Elise Lemire, Mark Flynn, and Martin Hewitt for their thoughtful and generous criticism.

The circulation of American slave narratives forms part of the general commercialization of American abolitionism in England. The African-American men and women who journeyed to England to escape the tyranny of the Fugitive Slave Law or to promote the struggle to abolish American slavery found themselves in demand: to lecture on their ideas about slavery, to display their black bodies and any personal scars which might bear testimony to the torture of American slavery, and to tell their stories. English desires to see and hear all about American slavery were nearly insatiable, and African-Americans found themselves constructed as just so much more abolitionist "product," consumed by English audiences who could not get their fill of "Uncle Tom," no matter what shape or form he assumed.

This time, however, the "Uncle Toms" on the page were not the product of either a sympathetic white Northerner or an antagonistic and politically calculating anonymous author. The slave narratives offered African-American men and women an opportunity to speak their minds, if only through the medium of words on a page. But would the "ladies of England" distinguish between the story of Frederick Douglass's life and Harriet Beecher Stowe's creation of "Uncle Tom"? Would "authentic" slave narratives pose any challenges for Victorian readers that fictional tales of slavery had not?[3]

In "Who Read the Slave Narratives?" (1959), Charles Nichols emphasizes that ante-bellum Americans from every walk of life read these slave tales. For Nichols, the question "who read the slave narratives?" gives way to "why did Americans read slave narratives?": what did readers see in them and how can we explain their immense popularity? Basing his conclusions on "Narratives of Fugitive Slaves," an essay by the pro-abolitionist Reverend Ephraim Peabody, published in 1849 in the American *Christian Examiner*, Nichols formulates his answers. Paraphrasing Peabody, Nichols concludes that "pictures of slavery by the slave" were calculated to, and did, exert "a very wide influence on public opinion" because they are "a vivid exhibition of the force and working of the native love of freedom in the individual mind" (149). In addition, Nichols concedes, slave narratives may have garnered some of their popularity from "sensationalism." The presence of "thrilling incident" in the narratives, Nichols explains, coincided serendipitously with "the nature of the age," an elliptical reference to the nineteenth-century American appetite for sensation. Finally, however, Nichols attributes the popularity of the genre "to the timeliness of the narratives." "Slav-

ery," Nichols writes, "was the most widely discussed and crucial problem of the age. No American could regard the matter with indifference,
even if he were not a slave-holder or an abolitionist" (152).

Why did Victorians read the slave narrative? Certainly, as in America, the timeliness and violent excitement of the narratives undergirded
their appeal in England. And, as in America, questions of slavery and
the abolitionist movement dominated public discourse and public interest in mid-Victorian England. As we have discussed already, massive
popular appeals had backed the Parliamentary reforms of the previous
years: the abolition of the slave trade (1807), of colonial slavery (1833),
and of colonial apprenticeship (1838). Douglas Lorimer writes that "The
anti-slavery movement in its attempt to persuade Parliament to abolish
the slave trade, and then slavery, organized one of the earliest and most
successful campaigns to arouse public opinion" ("Bibles, Banjoes and
Bones," 33). From 1839 through 1861, despite political rumblings about
decreased sugar production and political discontent in the West Indies,
and despite the renewal of outspoken racism symbolized by Carlyle's
widely disputed "The Nigger Question" (1853), the world-wide abolition of slavery remained a dominant cause in England.[4]

Under the politically acceptable mantle of abolitionism, then, the
slave narrative offered Victorian readers the excitement for which they
were eager: graphic scenes of torture, murder, sexual violence, and the
thrill of escape. G. Legman writes of the "century-long debauch of
printed sadism" (*Love and Death*, 11). Murder and violence were staples of
the English press, from "broadsides, ballads, 'last dying speeches' . . .
editions of the *Newgate Calendar*, a compendium of accounts of famous
murder trials [to the] Sunday papers [which] specialized in vividly
written stories of violence or scandal" (Altick, *Deadly Encounters*, 7).[5]

The titillating entertainment of the narratives was also clothed in the
morally acceptable fabric of the Christian odyssey tradition. As Blackett
writes, the narratives

> could all have been subtitled "The Progress of the Poor Fugitive," for they
> employed the traditions of the odyssey so popular in nineteenth-century litera-
> ture. Like the pilgrims in Bunyan's *The Pilgrim's Progress* – a literary staple of the
> century – the fugitives were continually confronted by obstacles that tested their
> resolve, strength of will, and character. (*Building an Antislavery Wall*, 26)

The quest of these fugitives, the moral underdogs of a corrupt American
society, was reassuringly familiar to Victorians: a humble attempt to
achieve the spiritual uplifting of Christianity denied to African-

Americans in slavery. In other words, what might otherwise have been deemed degraded, if not pornographic, writing could be considered respectable; slave narratives, full of violence normally taboo within the literature read by respectable middle-class men and women, could be enjoyed without guilt.[6]

Such generalizations about why Victorians read slave narratives are appealing, but they are also over-simplifications. Slave narratives were both similar to a number of pre-existing Victorian genres, such as the rags-to-riches story or the emerging genre of sensation fiction, and wildly different from anything else in the Victorian literary marketplace. Furthermore, the differences among Victorian readers, of class, of region, of political and of religious persuasion, to name a few, were likely to have highlighted very different aspects of the narratives as the source of their appeal. A white English working-class factory hand might have read *The Narrative of the Life of Frederick Douglass* as an uplifting story of a poor man's struggle to overcome social barriers and adversity in the quest for selfhood; in other words, beyond sensationalism, the worker's identification with Douglass and with Douglass's struggles might have formed part of the appeal of the narrative. In contrast, a white middle-class English Quaker might have found Pennington's narrative a fulfilling tale of the achievement of religious truth, identifying with Pennington's religious alienation from mainstream society. The simple variety of Victorian readers underlines the difficulty in trying to generalize accurately about why Victorians read American slave narratives.

Studying reactions to slave narratives in the form of contemporary reviews in a range of mainstream English periodicals and newspapers, however, we can refine our earlier generalizations. Reviews provide access not to the precise meaning of those narratives for all Victorians, but to the constellation of Victorian social concerns assigned to the event of the circulation of American slave narratives by the nineteenth-century periodical press. Moreover, as public discussions designed to teach readers how to make sense out of American slave narratives, the reviews worked to formulate and construct the texts as well as the terms of debate around the texts for many Victorians. Thus the reviews speak beyond the narrow domain of their predominantly white, male, middle-class authors.

I focus, in particular, on John Brown's *Slave Life in Georgia*, one of the many narratives published in London. An "as-told-to" narrative,[7] *Slave Life in Georgia* was "very heavily edited" by L. A. Chamerovzow, the

secretary of the British and Foreign Anti-Slavery Society, who claimed
the narrative was "written under [Brown's] dictation [and] as nearly as
possible in the language of the subject of it" (qtd. in Starling, *The Slave
Narrative*, 183). Chamerovzow's editorial role in Brown's narrative ren-
ders *Slave Life in Georgia* a problematic text in African-American literary
history[8] (although Marion Starling finds the narrative has "an authentic
ring, substantiated by the mass of records" [184]). Still, the narrative is
generically representative of the other slave narratives published and
circulated in England. Moreover, Chamerovzow's involvement seems
to have contributed to the visibility of the narrative, increasing advertising of the work and figuring in the widespread critical attention the
narrative received in the periodical press. Thus Chamerovzow's relation to the text, for our purposes, both makes its reception a bit more
accessible and magnifies the significance of that reception. Finally, *Slave
Life in Georgia* is the subject of my focus because the narrative contains a
fascinating internal critique of its own co-optation by the English press.

As the sneering comment about the interest of English women in "those
dear blacks" with which I began this chapter attests, not everyone
approved of Victorian consumption of slave tales. The *Athenaeum*, in a
review of John Brown's *Slave Life in Georgia*, took its stand among
Victorian periodicals in launching a complaint against this new genre of
texts. While crediting Brown as "an enterprising character [who] writes
in no bitter spirit, and is evidently solicitous to keep within the limits of
the truth [in his narrative]," the *Athenaeum* protests against the circulation of the narrative and against the current proliferation of American
slave narratives. The journal's protest is lodged as disapproval of the
way slave narratives function as literary texts: "There is too little variety
in these Slave-narratives to render their multiplication necessary. The
severities of masters, incarcerations, escapes, captures, floggings, and
excessive task-work, occur in one as in another, and we scarcely see how
the public is to be instructed by repetitious accounts so piteous and so
harrowing." The premise behind these sentiments is that the public
ought to be "instructed" by literature; hence the narratives do not
function as they ought to. Additionally, the review singles out for
disparagement the repetitious portrayal of violence in the narratives.
Eschewing the question of the pleasure the Victorian reader might
receive from the repetition of "harrowing" and "piteous" severities,[9] the
Athenaeum bemoans and dismisses the laceration of the reader's feelings.

The *Athenaeum*'s complaint in this review is levelled not just at the dysfunction of the narratives, but also at the way in which the narratives participate in and help to construct a literary marketplace based not on morality but on the demands of the reader. The reviewer writes that "Of course, if the fugitives find a market for their stories, they have a right to deal in them; but we can promise our readers nothing more than the stereotyped account of horrors, and nothing less than sickening amplifications on the effect of the bull-whip and the cobbing-ladle." While clearly finding the texts improper, the "wrong" kind of literature, the reviewer here acquiesces to the "market" and begrudges to the authors of slave narratives "a right" to "deal" their stories. Slave narratives, according to this vision, are texts hawked, like any other ware, by authors selling their writing. While the *Athenaeum* pronounces the "right" of such texts to circulate, it clearly laments the fact that questions of right or wrong, particularly of the morality of literature, have been eliminated in this new market in which the desires of readers, not the opinions of highbrow literary journals such as the *Athenaeum*, dictate the circulation of texts.

Enacted in the *Athenaeum* on the site of the circulation of American slave narratives, then, the conflict is between two literary economies: a literary market driven by readers' demands versus a literary market controlled by a cultural elite adjudicating the purpose and morality of literature for the masses. The proliferation of slave narratives, to the chagrin of the *Athenaeum*, evidences the existence, even the predominance, of the former market.

The battle over the different economies of the literary marketplace is heightened by the fact that the *Athenaeum* disdains the (desires of) readers who make up the "market." The journal cordons off a set of people, "our readers," whose taste and culture distinguish them from the masses.[10] The slave narrative reader, metonymic for the reader in the "market," is content with "stereotyped account[s] of horrors" and, worse, is a seeker of "sickening amplifications." "Our readers," insists the *Athenaeum*, do not participate in the literary marketplace in which readers' desires are pandered to by authors dealing their wares. The *Athenaeum* may concede to the authors of slave narratives "a right to deal" in the literary market, but the review makes clear that, by its high standards of literature and culture, the taste of most readers has been found wanting and the authors of slave narratives are likewise wrong to "deal" their texts to this audience. (That the *Athenaeum* would review this book, so obviously inappropriate by their own terms for its readers, only drives home the fact of the slippage between these two literary markets.)

The *Athenaeum*'s dismay with the "multiplication" of "stereotyped account[s] of horrors" in the form of slave narratives currently circulating within the literary marketplace resonates with the *Spectator*'s disgust at the commercialized consumption of *Uncle Tom's Cabin*, the "mob . . . rushing to see the leading personages [of *Uncle Tom's Cabin*] placed in a visible shape before its eyes" ("The Theatres"). In both cases, bitterness is not aimed at the anti-slavery cause but instead directed at the monstrously uncultured consumption of these abolitionist products by the "mob." The existence of a "market" in which a "mob," with its uncultured ways, can predominate is at the root of the problem. The *Athenaeum*'s review of *Slave Life in Georgia*, like the *Spectator*'s discussion of theatrical productions of *Uncle Tom's Cabin*, is transformed into a discussion, not of the "text" in question, but of the state (of disarray) of the Victorian literary marketplace, of the degraded taste of Victorian readers, and of Victorian society.

As Leslie Marchand argues, "the *Athenaeum* was the clearest and most unwarped mirror of [middle-class] Victorian culture among the periodical publications of the nineteenth century" (*A Mirror*, 167). The *Athenaeum*'s anxieties about the literary marketplace, then, should be seen not as isolated, idiosyncratic hysterics but as representative of larger middle-class anxieties about historical changes in the economy of the literary marketplace and in the culture generally.

The popular literary marketplace, once dominated by didactic fiction sponsored and controlled by the middle class for explicitly political purposes, was a thing of the past. According to Douglas Lorimer:

> Until the middle decades of the nineteenth century, literature of all kinds remained costly, and served a largely didactic purpose. Outside of political pamphleteering, popular literature originated largely with middle-class philanthropic sources, and aimed at teaching the lower orders [middle-class versions of] the lessons of moral improvement and self-help. [In the 1850s and 1860s and with] the rising of the standard of living among the literate population, new forms of popular entertainment and amusement emerged. A new cheap popular fiction appeared which aimed not to teach, but to entertain. ("Bibles, Banjoes and Bones," 34)[11]

As Colin Watson writes, "the production of books – their writing, printing and selling – had become a commercial operation, subject to commercial laws and pressures, and . . . their character was no longer likely to be determined by enlightened arbiters" such as the *Athenaeum* (*Snobbery with Violence*, 22). For the critics, the arbiters of the past, the irritation is not just that the masses are now influencing the shape of the literary market. Watson suggests as well "a sense of outrage" on the part of the critics "that people able to afford books, and therefore a cut above the plebeian masses, had neglected to show discrimination proper to their social standing."

Slave narratives were not unique in being cited as examples of consumption by a degraded readership. But this new situation in the literary marketplace in the middle decades of the century enabled and thrived on the circulation of the products of abolition such as slave narratives or, as we saw earlier, *Uncle Tom's Cabin*. The circulation of "slave tales" whose contents combined the morally and politically acceptable doctrines of abolition with less acceptable depictions of violence, sexual abuse, and "thrilling" plots (to say nothing of the portrayal of social upheaval in the narratives) epitomized the challenges posed to the middle class, particularly middle-class critics, by the dynamics of this new marketplace. The *Athenaeum*'s attack on Brown's *Slave Life in Georgia* can thus be seen as an aggressive attempt to meet and forestall these new challenges.[12]

If the displeasure articulated by the review in the *Athenaeum* at the demand-controlled economy of the literary marketplace was not rare, the discomfort it exhibited at the circulation of slave narratives was. For example, the *North and South Shields Gazette*, reviewing *The Narrative of William W[ells] Brown*, notes, in contrast to the *Athenaeum*'s queasiness: "we would that a copy of this narrative could be placed in the hands of every man in the British empire. No one who reads it but must rise up impressed with the conviction that slavery is an abominable thing." Likewise, the publication of Samuel Ringgold Ward's *Autobiography of a Fugitive Negro* was greeted with enthusiasm by the *Anti-Slavery Advocate* particularly because of its ability to penetrate the mass market which the *Athenaeum* so scorned:

We are . . . glad when anything appears in the shape of a book, which may assist in diffusing the principles of the abolitionists; or, even in a secondary way, bring their objects and efforts before the notice of the British public. It is more likely to be bought, read, and diffused among all classes than the anti-slavery newspapers, tracts, and reports, which . . . are not likely to attract the notice of the mass of readers.

While the *Athenaeum* sees in these texts the degradation of the Victorian reader and the disarray of the Victorian literary marketplace, the *North and South Shields Gazette* (a local newspaper), the *Anti-Slavery Advocate* (a national Garrisonian anti-slavery periodical) and a wide range of other Victorian periodicals[13] see the slave narratives as repositories of Victorian values, as I will show below. These periodicals can endorse the narratives and celebrate the literary marketplace because they redirect the *Athenaeum*'s anxiety about the English reader. The majority of Victorian periodicals, in reviewing slave narratives and sometimes directly responding to the concerns raised by the *Athenaeum*, find in the narratives not the pornographic appeal of a common literature for the common man but the violence of an inferior American world.

The aforementioned review of Ward's *Autobiography of a Fugitive Negro* in the *Anti-Slavery Advocate* is typical[14] in its emphasis on the violence of the narrative: "We could easily fill our present number with racy and telling extracts from its pages." The "terrible details" of slave narratives are viewed by the *Anti-Slavery Advocate*, however, not as "stereotyped account[s] of horrors," but as "intensely interesting." The paper even concedes that Ward's narrative is less interesting because it has fewer violent details: "This volume . . . does not profess to give any of those terrible details of personal experience which makes the narratives of Douglass, Wells Brown, and Solomon Northup, so intensely interesting." The emphasis, in the *Anti-Slavery Advocate*, however, is not on the presence in the narratives merely of violence and cruelty; the emphasis is on the violence of American slave society and the cruelty of the United States. Ward's narrative is singled out not just for its portrayal of the "terrible details of personal experience" but for its demonstration of the violence in America: "we know of no other *book* which portrays with such telling effect the cruelty and contumely exhibited towards the people of colour in the United States" (original emphasis). Cruelty and contumely (towards blacks) are the condition of an objectified United States. The violence of Ward's narrative, in the *Anti-Slavery Advocate*, is singled out not as evidence of the degradation of the Victorian reader but as a measure of the wholesale degradation of the American nation. This strategy of straightforwardly advertising a slave narrative on the basis of its stocks of horrors while reading the violence of the narrative as evidence of American degradation is evident in many reviews.[15] The *Eclectic Review*, in a review of *Slave Life in Georgia*, is one of the many journals which directly addresses "our contemporaries" at the *Athenaeum*. The *Eclectic Review* remarks: "We dissent from this *dictum* [about the lack of variety in the narratives]. The sameness spoken of is good reason for the repetition. Men can scarcely credit the atrocities of the slave system, and the tale must be repeated again and again, in order that they may be aroused to becoming efforts for its suppression." Indeed, the *Eclectic Review* welcomes John Brown's narrative as "Another painful revelation from the dark prison-house of American slavery, over which our readers will do well to ponder." The atrocities of "the slave system," of "the dark prison-house of American slavery," and, by extension, the dark prison-house of American society are so terrible as to be unbelievable. Diverging from the *Athenaeum*'s dismissal of "the stereotyped account[s] of horrors" and "sickening amplifications" of torture, the *Eclectic Review* constructs the English reader's indulgence in the repeated violence of the slave narratives as a sign not of the reader's prurient taste but of the reader's noble efforts to come to terms with the "painful" horror of America.

The same process of interpreting the violence of slave narratives as evidence of American degradation and inferiority is involved in the *British Friend*'s similar rejection of the *Athenaeum*'s dismissal of slave narratives in another review of *Slave Life in Georgia*. "Some have said," the *British Friend* records, "we are tired of these narratives of escaped slaves. This feeling, we presume, has arisen from their frequent publication of late years." Taking issue with this sentiment, the *British Friend* recommends a "painfully-interesting volume," John Brown's narrative, which arouses "feelings of abhorrence of American slavery." There is much that varies from other narratives in *Slave Life in Georgia*, the *British Friend* tells readers: "the work . . . contains such details that are not exceeded, either in interest or atrocity, by anything within the pages of Harriet Beecher Stowe's world-renowned *Uncle Tom's Cabin*." With varied details of atrocity to induce disgust at American slavery and, by extension, American society, *Slave Life in Georgia* holds, according to the *British Friend*, new interest for its English readers.

A review in the *Herald of Peace* records that Brown's narrative "possesses a very deep and thrilling interest. It affords a glance of the irredeemable abomination of the slave system in America . . . which degrades man and dishonours God, and cannot long endure." Again, the degraded man, in this review, is not an English reader but an American, slave or free, degraded by his society's failings.

Slavery, as a review in the *Scottish Press* puts it, actually transforms Americans into savages. "Slavery [is] a thing of cruelty 'beyond compare'" in which the slaveholder is transformed by the violence of the institution: "we find not merely the treating of slaves as chattels [*sic*], but a ferocity engendered by the system, so that the cowhide and other instruments of torture were perpetually in demand, and punishments

measured out that more resembled true diablerie of savages than working the 'peculiar institution' of a land which declares all men equal."
The American's degradation by slavery is not shared by the English
reader, despite England's lack of declaration that all men are equal, for
the review concludes: "We warmly recommend the volume to all who
take an interest in slavery – and this, we suppose, is but another way of
describing the whole British people [who share] antipathy and . . .
opposition to a system so vile."

A brief review in the *Local Preacher's Magazine and Christian Family Record*
records the blow to American nationalism with a similar gibe at the
American "Declaration of Independence." The review decries *Slave Life
in Georgia*: "A narrative of soul-sickening wrong and oppression on the
part of the boasters of 'universal freedom,' which ought to excite the
indignation of every honest heart." It is unclear here which ought to
excite the indignation of the English subject more: the wrongful boasters
of universal freedom or the wrongful oppression of slavery. In any case,
"honest hearts" are possessed by English readers, if not by American
citizens. As Thomas Gossett writes (apropos of reactions to *Uncle Tom's
Cabin*), English reviewers "seemed to take equal pleasure in reacting
with horror to the evils [and horrors] of slavery and with something like
satisfaction to the fact that the American Constitution made the abolition of slavery virtually impossible" for those boasters of democracy
and universal freedom (*Uncle Tom's Cabin and American Culture*, 258).

The *Banner of Ulster* tells prospective readers that "John Brown pictures slave life as he experienced it . . . He details the privations and
sufferings of the cotton plantation . . . and the savage tortures which he
endured . . . and he concludes all with a graphic description of the
vicissitudes and perils" of his journey to freedom. To the review's
complacent voyeurism into American society, the *Banner of Ulster* adds a
peculiar chauvinistic twist about England's role in the American abolitionist movement: "Great Britain, so noted for its violence on the
subject of abolition, is the greatest supporter of slavery, by giving the
highest value to its products . . . Thus 'King Cotton' reigns supreme, and
millions contribute to his supremacy who profess to regard him as a
despot." While the adventures of (slave) life in America serve as a foil to
English superiority, the review also emphasizes that the power lies with
England, leader among nations "on the subject of abolition." If England
now supports "King Cotton," it falls within England's power to topple,
with a noble paternalism, the throne and tyrannical reign of "King
Cotton."

Such explicit confidence in England's ability to transform the American political landscape is also present in the review of Brown's narrative in *John O'Groat's Journal and Weekly Advertiser*. A short diatribe against slavery, "a bitter thing – a vile and unchristian institution . . . hostile to the genius and equity of the Christian faith . . . With this horrid institution we connect ignorance, depravity, and misery," is matched by the conviction that "a better day [is] at hand." While the narrative leaves unstated what part England will play in bringing about this better day, the review does emphasize English beneficence in the example of the effects of English influence on Canada. The review records that fugitive slaves are forwarded "from the land of bondage to Canada, where 'slaves cannot breathe' and where the mild spirit of British law is happily dominant." "It is a happy thing," the review concludes, "that there exists an asylum for such people, and that the rights of man are vindicated." England, more than slavery or John Brown, ends up being the subject and hero of this review: glorious England, whose influence extends even to the American slave constrained within the bitter evil of an American institution.[16]

Thus enlisted to do the work of Empire, the slave narrative is constructed in the reviews above as an indictment of America and as a vindication of English superiority. In the *Athenaeum*, the slave narrative catalyzes anxieties about the integrity of the middle-class, educated reader and his or her relation to uncultured, working-class "others" and serves as a focal point for distinguishing a literary marketplace controlled by a cultural elite from a capitalist, consumer-driven literary economy. The reviews above displace these anxieties about discord and degradation among the English by mobilizing a discourse of nationalism which distinguishes the healthy, noble English from their violent and degraded American "other."

Once again, given the long history of abolitionism serving to bolster English nationalism,[17] the eruption of nationalism on the site of slave narratives is no historical surprise. As the English came to believe that "Britain is best" and that the success of the Empire was due to a "cultural inheritance" (Weiner, *English Culture*, 42) unique to the English, English nationalism thrived on competition with America. Martin Weiner writes: "Just those characteristics anxiously perceived in . . . English society [were] projected across the Atlantic, where they could be more safely disparaged and repulsed . . . Disparagement of the 'American way of life' [could] help exorcise these spirits from English culture" (88–9). The violence of the "mob," bogeyman of middle-class Victorian

England, and the uncultured tastes of all Victorians which the new literary marketplace revealed and on which it thrived were, in other words, projected across the Atlantic onto the site of American slavery. Disparagement of the violence of American slavery, and hence of American society generally, could help to exorcise these unhealthy spirits from England and to cover over the internal differences that threatened the collective national identity of "Englishness."

If the story of the appropriation of the slave's pain and suffering in the service of English national interests is by now a familiar picture, I want to turn to one crack in this canvas. In particular, an incident in John Brown's narrative, the story of John Glasgow, muddies the ideological waters of English national superiority presented by the reviews above.

Glasgow, as Brown tells us in *Slave Life in Georgia*, "was a native of Demerara, born of free negro-parents." He became a seaman, travelling "to and fro to England, improving his opportunities so much that he saved money and was regarded as a prosperous man." Glasgow next "sought a wife," and found one "In the immediate neighborhood of Liverpool [where] there resided a small farmer who had a daughter." Explaining Glasgow's inter-marriage with a white English woman, Brown notes to his readers that, apart from material success, "John Glasgow was a fine fellow, tall of stature and powerful in frame, having a brave look and a noble carriage. The farmer's daughter married him with the approbation of her relatives." Next, having saved money, John Glasgow bought land, and "through the father's interest, [he] got into a small farm in the neighborhood and purchased . . . three horses, a plough and a cart" (188). Glasgow, as Brown emphasizes, perhaps to stave off future criticism, achieves his full standing as an English subject, acquiring a white wife (she and her family attracted in part by his success and his fine looks), a farm, and three horses.

As the father of two children, Glasgow takes to the sea once more, "under an English captain," on a vessel bound for Savannah. Arriving at Savannah, "By virtue of certain provisions of the Black Law of Georgia, though a free-born British subject . . . Glasgow was conveyed to gaol, and incarcerated until the vessel that brought him to the port should discharge her cargo, be re-laden, and on the point of sailing away." The ship is delayed; moreover, the Captain "has to pay high wages to the slave who had been hired to him to do John Glasgow's work." Finding "that the gaol fees for John's release had run up enormously high," Brown reports, "the captain refused to pay them and let sail without him" (189). "John Glasgow," Brown concludes, "was then taken out of the gaol and sold on the auction block for *$350* to Thomas Stevens, on whose plantation [Brown] found him" (original emphasis, 190).[18]

Glasgow's story epitomizes the encroachment of American slavery on English freedom and on English power. It underlines English conciliation to American rule: Glasgow's captain refuses to pay the gaol fees but also abandons Glasgow, passively acquiescing to Savannah's *de facto* enslavement of black visitors. Brown stresses the moral and political failure of the Captain, of the English government, and, by extension, of English society in this abandonment. Anticipating feelings on the part of white English readers that Glasgow is somehow less an English subject than a white sailor, Brown insists on Glasgow's claim with his inclusion of details from Glasgow's domestic life in England: white wife, land in England, horses, children.

Some reviews, however, pass over this particular horror of American slavery, symbolic both of the encroachment of slavery on English life and of English political and moral complicity in American slavery. A fairly lengthy review of the narrative in the *Wesleyan Times*, for example, makes no mention of John Glasgow's story. The review focuses, instead, on the "heartrending and distressing" story of John Brown, including an excerpt of Brown's punishment for "a venial offense" introduced to the reader as evidence that one of "Brown's master[s] was a worthy brother of Simon Legree in all that was fiendish and brutal." Unlike America, home to a family of Legree-like monsters, England is "the home of the free" for the *Wesleyan Times*, although such a construction requires the omission of Glasgow's lack of freedom and of Glasgow's Legree-like treatment by his English Captain. Obviously, the inclusion of John Glasgow's tale in a review of *Slave Life in Georgia* would complicate the construction of the narrative as evidence of English moral and political superiority.

Many reviews, however, manage to incorporate the disruptive tale of John Glasgow without disturbing the ideological construction of the narrative. The *Hastings and St. Leonards News*, for example, notices for its readers the story of the "seizure, enslavement, and torturing of John Glasgow, a free-born British subject, having a wife and family in the neighborhood of Liverpool." Concluding that "We are shown [in the narrative] how a free British subject can be made a slave in strict accordance with American law," the review abandons this brief (one sentence's worth) attention to the effects of slavery on an Englishman and passes without comment from the kidnapping of Glasgow into American slavery to the question of English consumption of "slave-grown products." Ignoring the politically loaded question of the enslavement of a fellow-English subject, the reader is urged to concentrate on his or her own political strength, his or her ability "to drive the slave-owner from all hope of finding profit in slave-grown produce." Having displaced the question of John Glasgow's enslavement in America onto the relatively neutral issue of the English boycott of slave-grown products, the *Hastings and St. Leonards News* can continue to recommend John Brown's book as "a thrilling narrative [which] show[s] some of the terrible cruelties inflicted on the wretched slaves [and] provides the reader with some important facts as to the *refinements* of this hateful system" (original emphasis). Once again, the English reader's entry into this book of cruelty is rendered acceptable by turning the focus onto the degradation of American society: "the accursed system of slavery eats like a canker-worm into the vitals of American society, and becomes yearly a more glaring eyesore in the face of Heaven." For this reason, the review can conclude, in still another allusion to the *Athenaeum* and to the character of the English reader: "surely it is *not* invariably a right moral feeling to turn from the narrative of a fellow-creature's suffering, even when the tale revolts the feelings" (emphasis added). Yet the *Hastings and St. Leonards News* turns from the suffering of fellow-English subject and fellow-creature, John Glasgow.

The *Christian Weekly News*, similarly, attempts to incorporate the disruptive tale of John Glasgow into a construction of the narrative as a paean to the English Empire. Its review records the "affecting and instructive" story of Glasgow: "never did one country commit outrage upon another more flagrant than America in this instance upon England, in the person of her citizen, John Glasgow." Indignation about America's misbehavior in this instance is balanced, however, by a following discussion of John Morgan, a Scotsman also mentioned in *Slave Life in Georgia*, who "settled in Georgia as a planter on the principle of employing only free labour." Facing the "jealousy and hatred of the whole community," Morgan nevertheless "prospered." This model English citizen, as the review records, "told [Brown] that there was a land where the black men, if well conducted, would meet equal respect – that land was England." America's outrageous treatment of John Glasgow is set against the example of Morgan, the noble Scotsman, who conducts his business in an estimable, and estimably English, way and praises the lack of racism and the wealth of liberty in England. The story

of John Glasgow, then, fades into the background as the review converges on the foreground of English enlightenment and the superiority
of English capitalism.

One review seems to escape this cycle of blame and self-righteousness
on the part of the English, focusing extensively not just on Glasgow but
on English complacency about his position. The *Empire*, an abolitionist
magazine edited by George Thompson, describes the "painful story of
John Glasgow" and asks:

Why has not the British Government demanded of the constituted authorities
of the state of Georgia the restitution, if he be living, of John Glasgow? Why
does it not demand (and heap remonstrance upon remonstrance if the demand
not be complied with) the abrogation of a law which lowers the coloured
subjects of Queen Victoria, to a level with slaves? And why, also, does it happen
that the people of this country, who express so much sympathy for the Poles
and Hungarians, should, as far as active effort is concerned, be indifferent to the
wrongs of their coloured fellow-citizens, who are confined in the gaols of
Charleston or Savannah, and who are even exposed to the terrible fate of John
Glasgow?

With its straightforward attempt to face the contradictions within the
neat façade of English abolitionism and superior world leadership, the
review of *Slave Life in Georgia* in the *Empire* seems to be the exception that
proves the rule. Slave narratives, as they were constructed by reviews in
Victorian periodicals, were not, finally, read as stories posing the moral
complexities of American slavery to English readers.

It should come as no surprise that the English public would be uncom-
fortable with John Glasgow's story; betrayed, more or less, by his
captain and his country, this English subject remains an anomaly for
English readers who wish to enjoy the reassuring indulgences of tales of
American slaves, *American* slavery, and *American* hypocrisy and corruption.
The (lack of) reaction to the story of John Glasgow in reviews of John
Brown's narrative reveals the degree to which the slave narrative, like
Uncle Tom's Cabin and *Uncle Tom in England*, was constructed as a
transatlantic product, meant to highlight English national identity. It is
finally the nature of the white English subject, not his black brother, that
was grafted onto, and argued over in, reviews of these texts of abolition.

I began this discussion with the disclaimer that reviews do not provide
access to the precise meaning of the narratives for all Victorians. The
gap between the shaping of these narratives by Victorian periodicals as
texts of nationalism and the ideological work they actually performed

remains. The construction of the narratives cannot be taken as mono-lithic and unfractured. The fact that many reviewers express dissatisfac-tion with the ways in which they perceived the narratives were being read suggests that some Victorians may have been consuming the narratives differently. Did some Victorian readers eschew the ideologi-cal constructions of the periodical press? Did some, along with the *Empire*, see John Glasgow's presence in the narrative as haunting and disruptive? What other Victorian issues and debates were read in and through these texts by Victorian readers? We cannot be sure.

What we can be sure of is that American slave narratives were read by Victorian reviewers within the contexts of available popular discourses. Drawing on the cross-currents of Victorian society, these tales of slavery were seen as the newest site for fears about the emerging Victorian literary marketplace, new Victorian readers, and the general degrada-tion of English men and women. But these same anxieties about disturb-ances within the nation and within the characters of (some of) the men and women who composed the nation were also allayed when these texts were mobilized by a public discourse of nationalism and read as tales of American inferiority and English superiority. In the end, what is clear is that Englishness was, at this moment in time, a fragile and contested identity. And American slavery was one ground on which an emerging mid-Victorian English identity could be contested, re-worked, and ultimately re-forged.

John Brown may have anticipated the self-serving way in which his narrative would be read in England. The inclusion of the tale of John Glasgow may have been Brown's attempt to pre-empt and forestall such an appropriation of his life story. If so, it is not clear if his effort was at all successful. Perhaps the men and women who actually travelled across the Atlantic and spoke their own words to English audiences would find it easier to resist the ideological pull to which African-American charac-ters on the page, from "Uncle Tom" to "John Brown," seemed to succumb.

CHAPTER 4

"Negrophilism" and nationalism: the spectacle of the African-American abolitionist

The mother country, of late years, has signalized itself particularly in the great delight it has taken to avail itself of every opportunity to foster, and feed, and flatter, runaway American negroes. It has long been a standing joke, among the witty and satirical writers of England, their own countrymen's fondness for lions and lionizing, – a taste that has formed the theme of much deserved ridicule, and that has furnished a point to no little humour. Persians, with longbeards, – Turks, with long pipes – Chinese, with long tails, and North American Indians, with *not very long* blankets, are constantly succeeding one another in the *salons*, or at the tables of the *haut ton*, – one monster lion yielding place to the other, and, in time, receiving the delicate attentions of the fair, the services of the powerful, and the admiration of all.

But throughout all this Britonnia [*sic*] is a little fickle in her fashions, and, having run from the delicate Chinese olive, down through the dark-hued Asiatic, and Turkish, and Moorish, and copper coloured Indian, she has lately discovered, in the indulgence of her singular taste, that in this matter of complexion, – "in this deepest deep, a deeper still" of hue. Nothing goes down, now, with her, so well as the genuine black. ("English Negrophilism")

It might seem surprising to begin a discussion of the presence of African-American abolitionists in England with such an exaggerated and ungenerous parody of that presence. Yet this bombastic notice, entitled "English Negrophilism," first published in the American *New York Express* and reprinted in the English *Anti-Slavery Standard*, offers a compelling reading of the English public's "delight" in "runaway American negroes." Notwithstanding the American author's racism,

Material from this chapter was presented to audiences at the American Studies Association meetings in Washington, DC. For thoughtful comments, I am grateful to the audience, members of the panel, as well as Donald Gibson, Leslie Harris, and Jean Fagan Yellin. For thoughtful and generous criticism, I also want to thank Chris Hosgood, my two anonymous readers at *Victorian Review*, and Karen Jean Hunt.

xenophobia, and his formidable axe-to-grind, this article lays bare the mid-Victorian obsession with "monster lion[s]," exotic "others" of different "hue[s]" and "complexion[s]."[1] American blacks, from Frederick Douglass to Ellen Craft to Henry "Box" Brown, came as representatives of the transatlantic anti-slavery campaign, but they also took their places in a parade of non-white Others, each displayed in "its" objectified turn in front of the English public as an exotic spectacle.

For the writer at the *New York Express*, it is this exotic spectacle, not political affiliation or ideological sympathy, that defines the demand for and popularity of these African-Americans throughout England. The article charges that London

literally swarms with the race. All the public places are as vocal with them as a growing cornfield with crows, or a patch of barley with blackbirds. Ethiopians of every shade are so greatly in vogue, that the whites – men, and women, too! – are colouring their faces and hands, and going about London imitating their sable visitors, who, however, being the genuine thing, are bringing of their pockets full of money, the proof of John Bull's enlarged negrophilism.[2]

The grotesque caricatures invoked here discredit and defame African-American abolitionists and their activities in England. But Victorians really did want Frederick Douglass's company for tea and his profile for mezzotint, just as they had wanted to read his narrative. The English penchant for the "genuine" black ranged from the street and the music hall to "respectable" anti-slavery gatherings. Through lecture tours that varied along a continuum of pomp and politics, African-American abolitionists brought information about American slavery to people from all walks of life throughout the British Isles. From small towns such as Ledbury and Ventnor in Hampshire and the Isle of Wight to the major industrial centers such as Manchester, Birmingham, and Leeds, African-Americans spoke to groups ranging from a few to several thousand people. They spoke often; as Blackett records, "Douglass delivered fifty lectures in the first four months of his visit, the number rising by the end of his nineteen-month tour to three hundred" (*Building an Antislavery Wall*, 17). An appearance often involved more than just a lecture; while speaking about their personal life experiences and about the experiences of other black men and women in American slavery, the lecturer might present enormous panoramas depicting scenes of American slavery (none of which are known to have survived), reveal personal scars (Houston A. Baker has called these public displays of the physical markings of slavery the "Negro exhibit" [*Workings of the Spirit*, 13]), or display the instruments of torture used in slavery. Even in traditional anti-slavery circles, African-American abolitionists were, as C. Peter Ripley writes, "essential to the cause": the "attraction of rubbing shoulders with the black American abolitionists . . . had no substitute" (*The Black Abolitionist Papers*, 18).[3]

But the *New York Express*'s real target is not the activities of African-American abolitionists, although they bear the brunt of the author's wrath in this article. The ultimate target here is the English public.

The effect that this Anglican passion for blacks is having upon us at home, is getting to be somewhat alarming! Our plantations are in danger of utter depopulation, such is the demand for the "article" of Ethiopian lions in the London market. The fact of their having run away, materially advances the value of the importation, and if there has been a murder, or other little enormity attending the *escapade*, the popularity of the perpetrator is sure to rise in proportion. Exeter Hall is forthwith thrown open, for the holding forth of the new Apostle of Liberty. London Tavern smokes and reeks with feasts in honour of the "man and the brother" at which the "model republic" is roundly denounced and British love of liberty, proportionably exalted. All his movements are chronicled, all his sayings reported, his profile is done in mezzotint, and circulated, the old ladies invite him to their tea drinkings, and the young ones exclaim "what a dear!" Such was the excitement, (not a whit exaggerated,) created by the arrival of Fred [*sic*] Douglass in the British metropolis, and such . . . is likely to continue (till the "fashion" fades out) to be the case, at every new importation of blacks from this to the mother-country.

As this passage testifies, tensions run deep between the "mother-country" and its rebellious child over this "fashion" for Others. While the notice casts its complaint satirically, the mockery neither camouflages nor diminishes the stakes here. England, casting itself as the land of freedom, sloganeering that each visitor is a "man and [a] brother," competes with the United States, the land of surpassing democratic freedoms, the newly born "model republic." And even though American national security is not literally threatened by the "utter depopulation" of slave plantations, the popularity of visitors like Frederick Douglass in England represents a threat to America's national identity as the "model republic."

To meet this threat, the notice concludes with its most open slur on England by laying the blame for slavery at England's feet and decrying English interest in American fugitive slaves:

But perhaps, after all, we may take all these demonstrations of fondness for the blacks of this country, on the part of the English community, as intimation of a consciousness of their deep indebtedness towards the race. For, as it was England who first planted Slavery here, when we were her colonies, – where, in order to add to her revenue, she systematically laid the foundation of, and reared up, the enormous evil which she has bequeathed to us, – so it is fit and proper, and highly creditable to her, that she should now do all in her power to make the visits of these luckless victims of her policy as pleasant and agreeable as possible, whenever they see fit to lay claim to her hospitality.

English interest in American ex-slaves is here a grotesque parody of humanitarianism and enlightenment. The lionizing of American blacks is merely the hapless conclusion of English policy: once used to build the English Empire, these "luckless victims," feted and feasted, are now used to entertain the populace. Thus the *New York Express*'s reading of English interest in the African-American abolitionist campaign as a tale of hypocritical desire crossed with sensational delight is calculated to enable the paper and its readers to meet and defuse any challenge to America's national image. Whether or not the paper is an accurate barometer of English public opinion and popular culture, what is clear from this newspaper notice is that the lionizing of African-Americans in England sparked issues of both English and American national self-definition.

In other words, as non-fictional "Uncle Toms" like Douglass entered onto the scene in England, their presence and popularity, like that of their fictional counterparts, became a site of conflict. And while Stowe's fictional "Uncle Tom" may have initiated a cultural crisis by offering an unauthorized version of American slavery to Victorians, these "Uncle Toms" were not merely figures in the nation's imagination. *Uncle Tom in England* may have introduced a new "Uncle Tom" to challenge the Stowe original; slave narratives may have been pressed into the service of English cultural dramas. These "Uncle Toms," however, could speak their own minds. They were flesh and blood, not just words on a page. Could these men and women be pressed into ideological service as their written analogues, fictional or non-fictional, had been? Would the transgressive power of actual people prove more difficult to harness than that of a novel or a slave narrative?

I have chosen to concentrate on two contrasting figures, Henry "Box" Brown and Sarah Remond. Given the number of lecturers and the number of appearances each made, I obviously needed to narrow the field. My choices reflect the unusual and compelling particulars of these two stories. Henry "Box" Brown was the showman of the lecture circuit, whose buffoonery delighted and repelled English audiences, but he also had the temerity to sue a newspaper editor for libelling his character and his exhibition. The cultured and light-skinned Sarah

Remond forms a sharp contrast to "Box" Brown; she was one of only two African-American women active in the transatlantic lecture circuit. Unlike Ellen Craft, whose activities were overshadowed by her husband's and may have been impeded by duties to her children, Remond offered her audiences an independent, unfettered voice. Finally, my choices were influenced by the fact that, unlike Frederick Douglass or William Wells Brown, neither "Box" Brown nor Remond was at the forefront of nineteenth-century abolitionism. Thus, reactions to "Box" Brown and Remond are less reflections of English anxieties about the particular, exceptional power of black celebrities like Douglass and Brown and hence more representative of general reactions to the abolitionist campaign.

After escaping American slavery in a small box which was shipped from the South to the North of the United States in 1849, hence his name, Henry "Box" Brown came to England in 1851, fleeing the Fugitive Slave Law. He arrived in Liverpool in November, 1851, and commenced his career as a travelling lecturer. In the 1850s he spoke to audiences throughout England on American slavery; his exhibition, including various panoramic views "painted on 50,000 feet of canvas, by some celebrated artists of Boston" ("Untitled," *Preston Guardian and Advertiser*, Jan. 25, 1851), dioramas, and the singing of "native melodies" ("Untitled," *Preston Guardian and Advertiser*, Jan. 18, 1851), piqued Victorian curiosity and was widely successful.[4] Newspaper accounts of his work reflect his popularity and celebrate his abolitionist credentials, the truth of his lectures, the brilliance of his panorama, and the moral pleasure of his exhibition.

In May, 1851, "Box" Brown appeared at a music hall in Leeds. A notice in the *Leeds Mercury*, entitled "The Mirror of American Slavery," describes, with surprisingly little editorial commentary, his trip from Bradford to Leeds, a journey designed to re-play "Box" Brown's original journey out of slavery:

Mr. H. Box Brown, a fugitive slave, arrived in Leeds on Thursday evening from Bradford, packed in the identical box in which he first made his escape from slavery . . . He was packed up in the box at Bradford about half-past five o'clock, and forwarded to Leeds by the six o'clock train. On arriving at the Wellington station, the box was placed in a coach and, preceded by a band of music and banners, representing the stars and stripes of America, paraded through the principal streets of the town. The procession was attended by an immense concourse of spectators. Mr. C. A. Smith, a coloured friend of Mr.

Brown's, rode in the coach with the box, and afterwards opened it at the Music Hall. The box is 3 feet 1 inch long, 2 feet 6 inches high, and 2 feet wide. Mr. Brown's last "resurrection" (as he calls it) from the box took place at a quarter past eight o'clock, so that he had been confined in the space above indicated for two hours and three-quarters.

Completing his "resurrection" by literally emerging onto the music hall stage, "Box" Brown lectured briefly on his history, mainly his escape from slavery, and then exhibited his panorama, offering "for inspection a representation of the horrors of slavery in America."

The discussion of "Box" Brown's exhibition, particularly of his panorama, is less journalistically neutral:

The panorama is painted on 50,000 feet of canvass [*sic*], and comprises upwards of 100 views, including those of Richmond, Philadelphia, and Washington. In some of the tableaux are representations strikingly illustrative of American institutions and inconsistencies. The noble House of Congress stands at the top of one picture, and in the fore ground [*sic*] is to be seen a slave auction; also General Taylor (as President) driving in state into the city of Washington, whilst his four grey steeds are frightened by the cries and groans of a gang of slaves. The other scenes pourtrayed [*sic*] exhibit on canvass some of the freedom of America, with "heartless Knock-'em off" officiating as auctioneer, at a sale of what he calls "cattle (slaves) and other merchandise"; the celebration of the independence of America under the figure of liberty, and a sale of slaves going on at the same time; modes of capturing, flogging, torturing, and branding slaves; and notices in large letters, such as "Great sale of slaves of foreign and domestic production, in Liberty-square, near the Free Church."

While concentrating on the content and appearance of the panorama, the focus in this passage is on American "institutions and inconsistencies." As it is represented here,[5] the panorama converges into a series of taunts drawing together the "inconsistencies" of slavery with the icons of American democracy and American nationalism: the House of Congress, the President, the celebration of the independence of America, the figure of liberty. The "peculiar institution" serves as a synecdoche for the nation as a whole; criticism of American slavery in the panorama is launched as criticism of America itself. Figured in the panorama not as a problem for a few Southern individuals nor even for the South exclusively, slavery is thus presented as the defining problem of the American nation. In this way, without entering the thorny territory of the place of the African/slave character in a taxonomy of men or of the justifications of slavery based on arguments about its civilizing/Christianizing function, the panorama allows Victorians the simple pleasures of the ridicule it aims at America.

The tenor of this article is unsurprising, given the ways in which *Uncle Tom's Cabin* was read, at the expense of America, as the guarantor of English virtue. In fact, the *Leeds Mercury*'s reading of "Box" Brown and of his panorama of slavery is fairly typical. A notice on "Box" Brown entitled "Panorama of Slavery in America" in the *Bradford Observer* uses the same kind of inflated rhetoric to comment on the panorama's illustration of "the abominations and horrors of slavery, as it exists in the so-called liberty-loving states of America." To the English audience, "Box" Brown's exhibit is "striking and painful" in its depiction of "sufferings under this accursed American institution [which] never fail to rouse the just indignation and horror of true Englishmen." Englishmen, as the reception of "Box" Brown and of the cause of American abolitionism generally demonstrates, are just and true, unlike their American counterparts.[6]

Perhaps it was because "Box" Brown and his exhibition enforced their flattering self-constructions that Victorians flocked to his exhibit. In any case, there is little here to suggest that, with his acute sense of the sensational, "Box" Brown was doing anything other than clothing himself in the familiar trappings of national chauvinism that had been deployed to neutralize and defuse the transgressive possibilities of "Uncle Tom." A spectacular parade with a band of music and "American" banners on hand to underline the national roast hardly threatened the principles of Victorian society.

Yet not everyone was pleased with "Box" Brown and his exhibition. On March 17, 1852, the *Wolverhampton and Staffordshire Herald* attacked "Box" Brown, his lectures, and his panorama. The notice begins by stating that "Box" Brown's "representation of slavery is a gross and palpable exaggeration," his exhibition "a jumbled mass of contradictions and absurdities, assertions without proof, geography without boundary and horrors without parallel." Echoing *The Times*'s rejoinder against *Uncle Tom's Cabin*, the notice complains that exhibitions such as "Box" Brown's will not benefit the cause of abolition. Instead, the author insists, "Box" Brown and his exhibition are guaranteed to "generate disgust at the foppery, conceit, vanity, and egotistical stupidity of the 'Box' Brown school."

On top of this displeasure with "Box" Brown and his "very partial, unfair, and decidedly false view of American slavery," the notice also resounds with concern about the English public, again echoing *The Times*'s response to *Uncle Tom's Cabin*. Audiences for "Box" Brown,[7] the editor is dismayed to report, are "overwhelm[ed]" by the exhibition which they consume "wide-mouthed and wondergaping." Their susceptibility to "Box" Brown is compounded by the clergymen, respectable individuals, and the press. These standard bearers of public opinion have failed to discern correctly "Box" Brown's fraud. The editor complains:

> How clergymen and other respectable individuals, and even portions of the press, could lend themselves to such a juggle [*sic*], we do not know; but testimonials from such men (who doubtless received all "Box" Brown's descriptions as unmingled gospel), are read before the audience, and they are full of fulsome compliment to the bejewelled "darkey" whose portly figure and overdressed appearance bespeak the gullibility of our most credulous age and nation.

The failure of judgment by those members of society whose testimonials are meant to be trustworthy adjudications of respectability is a grave matter. For the editor of the *Wolverhampton and Staffordshire Herald*, "Box" Brown's fraudulent success exposes the fact that the nation of England is gullible, credulous, and, as was feared by *The Times*'s reviewer of *Uncle Tom's Cabin*, vulnerable to untoward cultural invasion.

Performing the duty that others have neglected, the editor takes up the tasks of saving the public from itself and its own bad taste and of restoring the good name of the impugned nation. The editor "deeply regret[s] that the public should be gulled" and "caution[s] those who may attend, to expect only amusement, as the horrors related in the richest nigger style are as good as pantomime." This coded warning actually delivers the final blow to "Box" Brown's credibility and ensures that a chastened public will not attend because English audiences would not be interested in a show that offers "only amusement." "Only amusement," without any accompanying education or instruction, would have rendered "Box" Brown's exhibition inappropriate for "respectable" people.[8] Richard Altick argues that "the desirability of 'rational amusement' – education sugarcoated with entertainment – became an article of social faith [to respectable, middle-class Victorians.] The search for the elusive acceptable balance between instruction and diversion became the recurrent motif . . . in the history of London exhibitions" (*The Shows of London*, 3).[9] This seems to be the case here where pantomime without purpose, as the editor well knows, is not suitable.

A notice in the following week's edition of the *Wolverhampton and Staffordshire Herald*, entitled "The 'Nigger' Panorama," makes clear that the editor's identification of the exhibition as "only amusement" served its purpose. The notice begins, as if with a sigh of relief, with the statement that:

> It is gratifying to hear that the good sense and discrimination of the inhabitants of Wolverhampton have led them to bestow such an amount of patronage, on this vile caricature of American scenery, as its inherent worthlessness and disgusting exaggeration so absolutely deserved. We learn from our reporters – for we have not ventured a second time to witness so foul a calumny *in colours* on the slave-holders of the Southern States – that the nightly attendance has been meagre in the extreme . . . his nocturnal antics [played] to the delight and merriment of the juvenile rag-a-muffins who for the most part make up the "darkey's" audiences.

To the relief of the newspaper, its previous notice served to re-instill English readers/exhibition-goers with "good sense and discrimination." With the "juvenile rag-a-muffins" who continue to patronize "Box" Brown's exhibition, the writer is unconcerned. These creatures obviously do not count among the "inhabitants of Wolverhampton"; their "delight and merriment" in "nocturnal antics" merely confirms their difference from the majority of the Wolverhampton public who, recognizing the fraud of "Box" Brown's exhibition or at least heeding the warning of the *Wolverhampton and Staffordshire Herald*, have, like the editor, not ventured forth again.

While the sanctity and dignity of Wolverhampton (and the English nation) is tentatively restored, the previous notice's description of "wide-mouthed and wondergaping audiences" and the "gullibility of our most credulous age and nation" lingers behind the current notice's assertion of the "good sense and discrimination of the inhabitants of Wolverhampton." Moreover, the association made in the *Wolverhampton and Staffordshire Herald* between "Box" Brown's exhibition and degraded but popular "antics," an association which exposes a dangerous vulnerability within the English character, continues to reverberate behind other discussions of "Box" Brown.

For example, the *Daily News* rehearses a similar argument about "Box" Brown in the midst of a flattering review of *Uncle Tom's Cabin* which distinguishes the "art" of Stowe's text from other debased "entertainment." The reference to "Box" Brown is introduced elliptically, as the notice differentiates between Stowe and the "refugee or emancipated slave appealing to the hollow and vicious sympathies of hypocritical Pharisaism, congratulating itself on virtue which was never tempted, reasoning instances as rules, and attempting to fix upon the whole of the slave-owners a character which, as a class, is not mainly applicable to them." Like the *Wolverhampton and Staffordshire Herald* and *The Times* before that, the article here raises the image of a Victorian audience with "hollow and vicious sympathies." Even after the writer completes his comparison between Stowe and "Box" Brown, the spectre of that audience remains. The notice explains that Stowe's "illustrations are not the exaggerations of Box Brown panoramas. She selects no hideous exceptional crimes of individual slaveholders. [She] rejects everything that could disgust needlessly or offend unjustly." By implication, then, "Box" Brown's panoramas show "hideous exceptional crimes," "disgust needlessly," and "offend unjustly." In other words, only those of "hollow and vicious" feelings would seek out such an offensive and disgusting exhibition.

So who are these unholy people? Remember that the editor at the *Wolverhampton and Staffordshire Herald* first conceded that they were everyone, including clergymen and respectable individuals, and then cordoned them off from the town's "inhabitants" as vagabond, "juvenile rag-a-muffins." The *Daily News* is less able to contain the disruption it invites with its allowance that the ex-slave holds an "appeal." "Hypocritical Pharisaism" – perhaps an allusion to English abolitionists, whose campaign for the abolition of slavery in the colonies was a "virtue . . . never tempted" and whose support for the anti-slavery movement generally betrays a hypocritical neglect of the English poor – does the work of the *Wolverhampton and Staffordshire Herald*'s "rag-a-muffins." But if this passage attributes "hollow and vicious sympathies" for the ex-slave exclusively to abolitionists, the dense grammar here works as a kind of deep cover, camouflaging but not eliminating the original spectre of a general Victorian audience whose sympathies are "hollow and vicious."

In both of these cases, then, what is clear is that "Box" Brown is being used as a symbol of what is wrong with Victorian society; vitriol aimed at him and his exhibition is meant to exorcise the unwanted within and to restore the town's inhabitants to their true and just, honorable selves. So far, "Box" Brown's experience in England is not all that different from that of his fictional counterpart, "Uncle Tom." Used either as a specter of English decadence to be exposed and exploded, as he is by the *Wolverhampton and Staffordshire Herald* above, or celebrated as a beacon of English national strength and integrity, as he is in the *Leeds Mercury*, "Box" Brown, like "Uncle Tom," serves contradictory ideological purposes. In the interstices between exhibition and spectator, the meaning of this abolitionist figure is produced and re-produced by newspaper editors twisting and contorting "Box" Brown's public image to fit the mold of a particular ideological agenda. While "Box" Brown's public persona may have been no less malleable than his fictional counterpart, notwithstanding "Box" Brown's literal body, there was some difference. Objecting to the way he and his exhibition were portrayed in the *Wolverhampton and Staffordshire Herald*, Henry "Box" Brown reacted as no fictional character could. He sued the editor for libel, and he won.

In a jury trial in Warwick on July 28, 1852, "Box" Brown sued the *Wolverhampton and Staffordshire Herald* over its representations of him in the two articles discussed above. He complained of a loss of income. He had "previously been in the habit of receiving from 50£ to 70£ a week," *The Times* reports in its "Summer Assizes" section, but "his receipts began to fall away immediately after the publication of the first libel." *The Times* records that "Box" Brown testified on his own behalf at the trial and "though his dress was rather fine, and he displayed some jewellery about his person, his manner of giving his evidence was quiet and creditable; and his pronunciation altogether very correct."

Both Douglas Lorimer and Richard Blackett view this incident, as well as *The Times*'s comments on "Box" Brown's appearance at the trial, as evidence of the "ridicule and abuse" (Lorimer, *Colour*, 54) and "more than just minor prejudice" (Blackett, *Building an Antislavery Wall*, 158) that African-American abolitionists faced. Certainly, this case is one of several which explodes the contemporary self-descriptions of England as a land free of the taint of racism. What was also at stake in the case was the role of the press as cultural arbiter for the nation, precisely that duty which the editor of the *Wolverhampton and Staffordshire Herald* had assumed in order to serve his community with his public defamation of "Box" Brown. The judge's directions to the jury, recorded by *The Times*, illustrate this point:

it was important that the right of public criticism upon books or other works should not be fettered or restricted; but when they [the jury] found observations made upon personal character they must weigh them with more rigour, because no man ought to attack the character of another without taking the utmost care to ascertain that he was right.

The importance of public criticism is primary here. The judge emphasizes that public criticism, performed by the press, "should not be fettered or restricted," presumably because it serves a vital role to the nation. But the judge distinguishes, and asks the jury to distinguish, between criticism aimed at texts and criticism aimed at people. In other words, the character of "Uncle Tom" could be attacked, as was the case in *The Times*'s own review of *Uncle Tom's Cabin* which performed its duty of warning the nation about the dangers of Stowe's novel; such criticism should not be restrained. An attack on "Box" Brown, however, would need to be held to a higher standard. Regardless of the nuances of this distinction (born out of a sense of the more serious threat to the English populace posed by texts rather than people?), what the judge affirms is the crucial importance of public criticism, unfettered in the case of criticism of books and carefully correct in the case of criticism of personal character.

In any case, this distinction was respected by the members of the white jury who found for "Box" Brown and awarded £100 in damages. But did this really represent a wholehearted victory? Had "Box" Brown withstood the attacks of the press and won? Had he been able to resist appropriation and mis-interpretation of his life and his works? A glance through the press's reactions to "Box" Brown's suit suggests how difficult it is to pronounce him a clear victor.

A reference to "Box" Brown in a review of *Uncle Tom's Cabin* in the *Morning Post* illustrates one way that "Box" Brown's libel suit was integrated into the Victorian imagination of him. A perusal of a new edition of Stowe's text, for the writer of this notice, "brought forcibly to our recollection [the] case" of Henry "Box" Brown. "The contrast between English liberty and American liberty," the notice continues, "could not be better illustrated" than by this case: "[after] the Fugitive Slave Bill became law, it was no longer safe for the poor negro to remain even in the most free districts of this land of liberty. To England, therefore, he came." Unlike "the most free districts" of the United States, England offers itself to "Box" Brown as the real "land of liberty." "Box" Brown's conflict with the editor of the *Wolverhampton and Stafford-shire Herald* in no way interferes with this delineation of facts. The *Morning Post* reports that the "editor of the local newspaper took offence at the exhibition; and, in his notices of the performance, not only criticized it with great severity, but largely indulged in personalities calculated to bring the exhibitor into ridicule and contempt." But, the *Morning Post* gleefully reports,

The escaped slave brought his action of libel . . . in a British court of justice he was examined as a witness – he told his own tale – his deportment produced a favourable impression upon the judge and the jury – and the black man, the fugitive slave, who had been hunted from the shores of America, recovered damages from the newspaper editor who had exceeded the fair bounds of criticism.

"Box" Brown's victory in an English court is the final proof of the "contrast between English liberty and American liberty" and confirms which nation is the true "land of liberty." "Box" Brown's ability to impress an English judge and jury testifies not to their debased taste but to their superior English judgment of fair play and justice (unlike their American counterparts who judge "Box" Brown as a man to be hunted). While for the editor of the *Wolverhampton and Staffordshire Herald* "Box" Brown's popularity in England represents the vulnerability of the English people, for the author of this notice in the *Morning Post*, "Box" Brown's capacity to gain the sympathy of an English court testifies to the superiority of the English nation. That the ridicule "Box" Brown had endured from the pen of an English editor could somehow end up as more evidence for a magnanimous assessment of English moral superiority seems an irony missed by the editor of the *Morning Post*. Once again, "Box" Brown's story, with a new appended ending in an English courtroom, comes wrapped in the uniform of English self-aggrandizement.

All this seems not to have bothered "Box" Brown. Notwithstanding his successful libel suit, he seems to have comfortably accommodated himself to the service for which he was destined and to the realities of his inevitable political appropriation. Combining his flair for the dramatic and his canny business sense, "Box" Brown's later exhibitions reveal a kind of callous complacency about any larger purpose for his work and expose the financial motivations which may have undergirded all his activities in England, even his momentary rebellion in the English courts.

An untitled article published on March 12, 1859, in the *West London Observer*, a local London newspaper, illustrates "Box" Brown's success in commodifying his sufferings for display in front of English strangers, in combining celebration of spectacle with English nationalism, but also in catering to the racism of that nationalism. Again, "Box" Brown enjoys great popularity: the newspaper records "crowds of spectators . . . The commodious room at the Town Hall was literally crammed; in fact, on Tuesday evening hundreds were unable to gain admission." A lecture by Mrs. Brown ("Box" Brown's new wife[10] who has come to participate in his exhibitions) is "listened to with breathless interest, and loudly applauded." In all, the *West London Observer* reckons, "Box" Brown "met with the utmost success."

In "giving an account of a most interesting entertainment which has been exhibiting at the Town Hall, Brentford, to crowds of spectators," the notice focuses on how "Box" Brown gives "a most vivid description of the horrors and cruelties" of American slavery as it is "carried on" by "the boasted Americans." Again, this entertainment, as viewed by the commentator at the *West London Observer*, confirms the superiority of England over America, despite the boasting of that nation, that confirmation no doubt underwriting the pleasure of the entertainment.

The article also records the changes in "Box" Brown's exhibition, commenting in particular on his display of a "grand original panorama of African and American Slavery":

["Box" Brown] has since added to his entertainment some dioramic views from the Holy Land, which are excellently painted, and ably described by Mrs. Henry Box Brown. Since the sad revolt in our Eastern Empire has occurred, Mr. Brown has had a panorama of the great Indian Mutiny painted, which he now exhibits alternately with his great American panorama, either of which affords a most excellent evenings's [*sic*] entertainment . . . To conclude the evening's entertainment on Wednesday, Mr. Brown, together with Professor Chadwick . . . introduced several experiments on mesmerism, human magnetism, and electrobiology, which proved most successful, and afforded the crowded audience much pleasure and amusement.

With interest in American abolition waning by 1859, was "Box" Brown forced to append to his presentation of American slavery artistic views of the Holy Land and depictions of the Indian Mutiny in order to maintain his appeal? The addition of "mesmerism, human magnetism, and electrobiology" suggests as much; "Box" Brown seems to be cramming all he can into his exhibition, with popular science offering one more draw for the audience. But the juxtaposition of abolitionism with the Indian Mutiny forms a paradoxical inclusion. The Indian Mutiny was replayed in England with "a general racist and political hysteria" (Brantlinger, *Rule of Darkness*, 202) in numerous essays, sermons, novels, poems, and plays: "according to the collective myth, the Indians had brutally massacred, in the most treacherous circumstances, English men, women and children" (C. Hall, *White, Male and Middle Class*, 282). By presenting panoramas depicting American Slavery together with scenes of the Indian Mutiny, lumping African-American slaves with the Indians who formed the very ogres of the Victorian imagination, "Box" Brown can only have played into a host of complicated English fears about non-white Others, himself included. That the commentator at the *West London Observer* does not find peculiar the combination in "Box" Brown's exhibit underlines that slavery *and* the Indian Mutiny offered "excellent . . . entertainment," "pleasure," and the "amusement" of spectacle. In this instance, such "entertainment" must have come not just at the expense of America and American nationalism but at the expense of African-American men and women.[11]

Was "Box" Brown's "entertainment" ever very different from the thousands of exhibitions of exotic spectacle which crowded Victorian popular culture? Was "Box" Brown merely one in a series of "monster lions" receiving the hypocritical attention of the English public?[12] It is clear that one of "Box" Brown's primary interests was, as the *New York Express* put it earlier, to make "pockets full of money." Yet "Box" Brown also seems to try to take control over and work his audiences, if only to establish himself as a successful and admirable entertainer whose exhibition could not be sabotaged without a fight. Still, "Box" Brown found himself a supporting actor in a larger drama about the state of the English nation, a drama played out variously as anxiety about English exhibition audiences and bravado about English national superiority. Even with control over his own words, "Box" Brown never controlled the play. But at least he did make for himself "pockets full of money."

Sarah Parker Remond was born to free black parents, Nancy and John Remond, in Salem, Massachusetts.[13] Her political commitment to American abolitionism continued that of her father, John Remond, a lifelong member of the Massachusetts Anti-Slavery Society, and her brother, Charles Lenox Remond, also an anti-slavery lecturer with transatlantic experience. As an agent for the American Anti-Slavery Society, she arrived in England in January, 1859, for a year-long speaking tour. She was widely successful, judging by attendance at her lectures – she spoke to a "crowded assembly" in Liverpool ("A Lady Lecturing"), to a "densely crowded" lecture hall in Warrington ("Miss Remond's Lecture"), to a room "crowded to excess" in Manchester ("American Slavery," *Manchester Courier*), and, in Leeds, to "1,000 persons" at tea ("Leeds Temperance Union").

Admission charges and descriptions of her audiences suggest that Remond's lectures attracted a slightly "better" class of people than "Box" Brown's.[14] Moreover, while newspaper accounts of "Box" Brown's appearances often read like considerations of the entertainment value of a show, the notices about Remond, usually containing long excerpts from her addresses alongside discussions of the occasion, are serious and considered.[15] Despite the respectability of Remond's lectures and the seriousness with which she is treated by the press, Remond inevitably constituted a spectacle for Victorians. Unlike "Box"

Brown, Remond used no theatrical props, no panoramas, no box, but her appearance itself on the lecture platform was enough to create a stir. As Barbara Taylor writes, discussing female lecturers within the Owenite movement, the "very presence of a woman on a public platform was guaranteed to raise popular interest" (*Eve and the New Jerusalem*, 140).[16]

The Mayor of Warrington raises this issue in his introduction of Remond to an audience in Warrington. As recorded in the *Warrington Guardian*, the Mayor observes that:

the lecturer was a lady, and however common that was in America, it was very uncommon here. Well, perhaps it ought to be. We in England looked to the past, to antiquity, to days gone by, and had found that it was not the manner of our country. But he could not forget that they had a lady on the throne, that ladies had risen to the highest rank of walk [*sic*] in literature and other paths, the only distinction being that they did not occasionally speak in public – not for a moment doubting their capability to do so – and therefore he did not see anything indecorous in a lady addressing them on the present occasion. ("American Slavery," Feb. 5)

Making an exception for Remond on "the present occasion," and arguing that such an exception is not "indecorous," the Mayor hints that the general practice of female lecturers *is* indecorous. England had carefully considered the practice of female lecturers, had "looked to the past," and had concluded that "it was not the manner" of the country. Women – Queen Victoria et al. – had achieved greatness; still the country eschewed women's public speaking. In other words, as we have seen so often before, Remond's presence becomes the occasion for a discussion of the difference between American ill-considered customs, which disgrace American society, and the superior manners and values of the English: Remond, as a female lecturer, stirs in the Mayor of Warrington a familiar bout of English nationalism.[17]

If Remond's gender provoked something of the expected reaction in the press, what is striking is that the nature of her subject matter did not. For in addition to being one of very few women and one of the first black women to lecture regularly before anti-slavery audiences, Remond was also one of the first white or black, male or female abolitionists to speak frankly and bluntly about the sexual abuse and sexual exploitation of black women in slavery. For example, one of the stories that recurred in Remond's lectures was the case of Margaret Garner. As recorded by the *Warrington Times* in an article entitled "Lecture on American Slavery by a Coloured Lady," Remond touchingly related the case of Margaret Garner, who determined to be free or die in the attempt. She was born a slave, and had suffered in her own person the degradation that a woman could not mention. She got as far as Cincinnati with her children . . . There she stood amidst magnificent temples dedicated to God on either hand, but no sympathy or help was afforded her. The slaveholder found her; as he appeared at the door she snatched up a knife and slew her first-born child, but before the poor frenzied creature could proceed further in her dread object, the hand of the tyrant was on her, when she called to the grandmother of the children to kill the others, as she preferred to return them to the bosom of God rather than they should be taken back to American slavery.[18]

Presumably such an explicit discussion of the violence within the system of slavery, including references to the sexual assaults on female slaves – "the degradation that a woman could not mention" – and the radically anti-maternal (in Victorian terms) attack of Margaret Garner on her infant, would be far more provocative and scandalous than the simple appearance of a woman on the lecture platform.[19]

But accounts of Remond's appearances in the Victorian press, while they regularly include passages from her lectures like the one above highlighting Margaret Garner's gruesome story, never so much as hint at the existence of voyeurism or sordid curiosity in Remond's audiences. Indeed, considering the reaction to "Box" Brown, the absence of any speculation about the "hollow and vicious sympathies" of members of Remond's audiences is a striking but revealing absence. Remond's audiences are regularly cast as philanthropically inclined, imputed to have the highest motivations for coming to hear her speak. At the same time, and despite the presence of excerpts such as the one above, Remond is consistently and remarkably transformed from an independent, vociferous advocate of women's rights and abolitionism who does not mince words to a civilized, cultured, lady, a "specimen of Victorian femininity" (McCaskill, "'Yours Very Truly,'" 523).[20]

The Mayor of Warrington's backhanded intimation of the "indecorous[ness]" of Remond's appearance on the lecture platform is in fact the exception. Nearly all commentary on Remond eschews this association and emphasizes instead "her truly lady-like manner" ("The Ladies' Meeting"). Remond, the English press insists, reflects all the qualities Victorian society cherishes in its women: cultivation, refinement, and modesty. In an article entitled "A Lady Lecturing on American Slavery," the *Liverpool Mercury* describes an address of an hour and a half by Remond, focusing on her feminine traits:

she retained the closest attention of her audience as she eloquently depicted the wrongs of the slave, dwelt in the most touching manner . . . expressed her unbounded indignation . . . and concluded with an earnest appeal . . . Miss Remond is an able advocate . . . she speaks strongly because she no doubt feels strongly upon the subject on which she speaks, and is eloquent because she makes no effort to be so. She has a clear, musical voice, a distinct utterance, and – if it be not a needless remark of a lady – we may add she has at her command a great flow of language, for she speaks without any assistance from notes . . . Her repeated quotations . . . display a retentive memory, whilst the whole of her address as plainly denotes that she has paid no little attention to general literature, and particularly to the writings of the poets of this and her native country.

With her "musical voice," "touching manner," "great flow of language," and "attention to general literature," Remond appears here as the model of an educated and refined English lady. A paragon of English femininity and virtues, Remond is, in other words, distanced from her violent, American peer, Margaret Garner, and read and accepted within the more genteel sisterhood of white English ladies. In the process of focusing on her lady-like qualities, such as her ability to quote English poetry, this account of Remond's lecture also manages to downplay both Remond's own words, including her oration on the wrongs of slavery, and the implications of her words for Victorian audiences.[21]

A comment in one article exposes some of the logic underlying this unabashed celebration of Remond as "truly lady-like" in these press accounts. The *Warrington Standard*, in a notice entitled "Lecture on American Slavery by a Lady of Colour," refers to Remond as "one of nature's nobility." In other words, like Rosetta and Marossi in *Uncle Tom in England*, Remond is a kind of noble savage. Even if she does not come directly from the "savage" land of Africa, Remond's cultivation, manners, and gentleness reflect that land's uncorrupted state of nature, and not the character of American blacks or of American society generally. In fact, Remond's identity is shaped by her difference from her American peers, her exceptionalness, and by the fact that somehow she has remained pure and untouched in the midst of the corruptions of American culture. Naming Remond "one of nature's nobility" allows the press to praise in Remond those aspects of womanhood valued by English society and thus to confirm the nobility of English womanhood generally.

In other words, like Henry "Box" Brown and like the fictional "Uncle Toms" before him, Remond is appropriated by the English press to serve pre-existing ideological needs. In the cases above, her appearance becomes the occasion for an affirmation of gender roles in English society and for a celebration of the values of the English Lady. This ideological work is facilitated by an apparently seamless identification with Remond on the part of her audiences. Unlike "Box" Brown, whose reception is marked by alternating sympathetic or hostile "othering," Remond's is structured around unbroken acceptance from English audiences. While "Box" Brown's "otherness" was apparently inescapable for English audiences, Remond is seemingly transformed into a nearly white, English lady whose "otherness" seems to go unnoticed.

This identification, however, exacts a cost. Remond is literally erased and remade in the image of an English lady by the periodical press. Yet Remond seems to resist this appropriation of her self. In her repeated invocations of Margaret Garner, Remond positions herself squarely within a black sisterhood and refuses to relinquish her racial identity to the needs and desires of the English press and people. Remond aligns herself with, and asks her listeners to do the hard work of feeling sympathy for, someone with whom they could not easily identify – a sexually abused black slave who defies the common values of motherhood by killing her own child. By choosing Garner's story as the centerpiece of her lectures, Remond challenges her audience's forceful attempts to assimilate her into their world.

Elsewhere, however, Remond seems to have been more shifty in her alliances. Another set-piece of her lectures invokes for Remond and her audiences a very different sisterhood, as an excerpt from an article entitled, "Miss Remond's First Lecture in Dublin," recorded in the *Anti-Slavery Advocates*, illustrates:

for the woman slave there was neither protection nor pity. If the veriest scoundrel, the meanest coward, the most loathsome ruffian, covets the person or plots the ruin of a defenceless female, provided she be known to be, ever so remotely, of African descent, she is in his power (sensation). Remember, this did not depend upon colour. She might possess the loveliness of a sylph; she might be endowed with the dignified beauty of a Cleopatra, or have the winning grace and charming innocence of a Juliet; she might be rich in every rare gift and accomplishment which can enhance female beauty; let her skin be white as alabaster, it has only to be shown that she holds even the remotest affinity with the proscribed race; it has only to be known that she is the child of a slave and a slave herself, she is liable to the brutality of the vilest wretches, and may be finally auctioned and sold at any time at the will of her "master."

Raising the specter of the ersatz white woman who is kidnapped into slavery to serve the vile desires of a low-class, lustful maniac, Remond positions herself and asks her audience to position themselves in a sisterhood not with all slave women but with the light-skinned exception, the slave woman who is really a white English lady save a few drops of blood. Certainly, this ploy is designed to muster support for the abolitionist cause. But by playing on a dynamic of English sympathy based on a racism of skin-tone and the prejudice of class, Remond musters support manufactured around the icon of middle-class white womanhood and wedded to a corresponding ideology of femininity. In other words, Remond may win sympathy for the anti-slavery cause, but she actually hinders the formation of a real alliance between her supporters and the many slave women who, like Garner, were not sylph-like or did not behave as if they were powerless and defenseless in the face of attacking white scoundrels.[22]

Moreover, having redirected the question of American slavery away from the example of Margaret Garner and back towards that of the woman of African descent with the beauty of Cleopatra, the innocence of Juliet, and the gifts and accomplishments of her white peers, Remond refocuses her audience's attention towards her own body and the visual image of her "white" womanhood. She plays into, in other words, an emphasis on her skin color and a de-emphasis of her more radical voice. This makes it all the more easy for Remond to be reduced by the periodical press to the fate typical of the African-American abolitionist: a nineteenth-century version of the poster-child for the English nation and English nationalism. Despite her voice, her ability to articulate the complexity of American slavery and of the abolitionist cause, her direct and explicit discussion of those aspects of slavery which might most transform her audiences, Remond is reduced to a pale caricature of herself.

This politically bleached version of Remond is often taken up by the English press as the most important subject for attention and analysis. So, for example, the *Warrington Guardian* comments on the idea that American society would enslave and degrade "a lady" like Remond:

> There she stood, a lady every inch: graceful, polished, educated so well as to quote our poets, recapitulate our most glorious battles, and speak of the deeds of our philanthropists with discrimination. We presume she is a free woman; yet in the land of democracy, under the Fugitive Slave Law, even in the Free States, upon the oath of any brutal fellow, to be carried into a bondage more fearful than that to which the most common negro is subjected. ("Slavery and Democracy")

Remond's ladylike appearances throughout England serve over and over again as evidence in a nation-wide indictment of America.

Indeed, just as it is the occasion for a comparison of the American custom of allowing female lecturers with the ancient and considered English custom of frowning on such behavior, Remond's presence serves as an opportunity for a full-scale comparison of English difference from and superiority to America. Unlike the Americans who might enslave this "lady," the English people receive her with respect: "The profound attention manifested by the audience and the intelligent response conveyed by every face, shewed [*sic*] that she was most fully appreciated" ("District News"). The press constantly reminds its readers of the uniformity of "correct" opinion in England on the subject of slavery: the *Warrington Guardian* insists that "England was unanimous on the subject of slavery . . . [and] the object of Miss Remond's lecture was to convince people on this side of the water that although we had not been agitating for some time past, still we had lost none of our old feelings on the subject" ("American Slavery," Feb. 5). The *Manchester Daily Examiner and Times* writes that "Deep regret was expressed that England had ever given up her right of search, as the African slave trade was fast reviving in consequence . . . Various details were given, which frequently elicited cries of 'Shame' from the audience" ("American Slavery").

English abolitionism, according to these periodicals, has led and continues to lead the way for freedom throughout the world. In contrast, according to the *Warrington Guardian*, "American slavery has done much to stem the tide of popular progress in Europe, and to uphold the iron rule of despotic kings. Men reason, and reason with truth, that if such things can be done in Republican America, with its vaunted Constitution, what might not be done in Europe if emperors, kings, and a hereditary monarchy were displaced?" ("American Slavery," Feb. 12). In another piece inspired by Remond's appearance and echoing *Uncle Tom in England*, the *Warrington Guardian* makes clear that England's role as the world's moral leader remains unchallenged, notwithstanding the so-called advances of the American Republic. Indeed, America's qualification for high rank among the civilized nations of the globe, unlike England's, lies only in "her commercial position":

We believe that wherever [America's] sin of influence is felt, it is destructive of pure morality and social affection, that the highest political greatness and religious development cannot be attained where it exists, and that the American nation can never arrive at that rank among the civilized nations of the globe which her commercial position so eminently qualifies her to fill until this evil is abolished from her dominions. ("Miss Remond's Lecture")[23]

A letter to the editor of the *Warrington Guardian* perhaps best exemplifies the costs of this re-making of Remond and of this response to her on a continuum of white, middle-class femininity rather than black sisterhood. Launching its attack not at American slavery but at American society, as so many of the notices cited above do, the author of this piece chastises a society which would allow such an encroachment upon and violation of (English values of) womanhood. Addressing the editor of the newspaper, the author suggests that in Remond, "the public may see one of a class of persons deemed only fit for slavery by the people of the United States; to whom they refuse the name of woman, and who, by the dictum of one of the first judges of that land, 'has no rights that the white man is bound to respect.'" One can imagine that the English public would hardly line up to see Margaret Garner, another of that "class" deemed fit for slavery and left vulnerable to the abuses of white men. The writer's invocation of Remond's "class" lays bare the underlying reasoning by which Remond's potential enslavement and defilement would be an unthinkable offense: her class.

Remond was part of a small circle of African-American abolitionists whose success lay, as Douglas Lorimer suggests, "in their ability to conform to conventions of correct behaviour" (*Colour*, 52). Unlike "Box" Brown, Remond was one of a group of visitors who

In manner, in speech, in dress, in their own confidence and social ease, and even in their mental outlook . . . were eminently qualified, and therefore acceptable in the best circles of Victorian society . . . The experience of eminent black abolitionists shows that the mid-Victorians did not treat all blacks alike. A fortunate few received the respect commanded by their abilities and their social accomplishments. (52–3)

Continually cast as a member of a "class" of eminent blacks, Remond enjoys unqualified access to and support from her audiences. She also gets marked as special, different, better than the other African-Americans who do not belong to that "class" and who are thus more rightfully subject to the horrors of slavery. At the same time, once identified as a Lady, Remond is immediately conscripted into the ideological battle of the English nation: an icon of white womanhood, Remond comes from the United States as a potent emblem of all that makes America inferior to its mother-nation, England. In the end, the radical potential of her message about the barbarity that slavery engenders in all who come in contact with it is diminished. More respected than "Box" Brown, Remond is, I think, more successful in initially resisting the pull of the inevitable national drama in which the English periodicals wish to cast her. Still, like him, Remond never controlled the play. Even when she spoke of Margaret Garner's violent acts, the critics noticed the tone of her voice more than the content of her words. In the end, Remond is as powerless as "Box" Brown over the public image constructed for her by the media.[24]

"How cautious and calculating":
English audiences and the impostor, Reuben Nixon

On December 26, 1845, addressing an anti-slavery meeting in Belfast, Frederick Douglass diverged from the subject of American slavery to speak about accusations being levelled against him.[1] An article entitled "Anti-Slavery Meeting" carried in the *Banner Of Ulster* records Douglass's remarks as follows:

[Douglass] craved permission to say a few words in reference to his own position. Attempts were being made to destroy his influence, by insinuating that he was not what he pretended to be, and could not exhibit any credentials from persons of respectability. He was, however, no impostor, and those who made the charge ought not to do so under the curtain, but in a public manner, and bring proofs to substantiate their allegations. He had been four months in Ireland, and delivered about fifty lectures, and never till he came to Belfast had he been asked for credentials. What a sensible people the inhabitants of this town are! How cautious and calculating, and what a prudent desire they evince for proceeding on sure grounds, lest they take a person void of respectability into their confidence! How circumspect about the character of the slave! But how about the Free Church? (Laughter and Cheers)

Whether or not the questions about Douglass's credentials, his character, and the authenticity of his status as an escaped American slave earned credence among the people of Ulster, Douglass does not seem to have allowed them to ruffle his feathers. He concludes this summation of the accusations against him by wondering whether the sensible inhabitants of this town are as prudent, cautious, and circumspect in all their dealings. In particular, Douglass asks his audience to compare their scrupulous suspicions of him with their acceptance of the Free Church: are the people of Ulster as cautious and circumspect about that institution as they are about Douglass? Since in this instance the audience seems already inclined towards Douglass and against the Free Church, Douglass's jab at the Free Church – his insinuations that this institution, and not himself, deserves the scrutiny of the people – meets with sympathy: the audience responds with "Laughter and Cheers."

So what is this exchange all about? The newly established Free Church of Scotland had sent a high-level commission to the United States to open contacts with American churches and raise money. Douglass alludes here to the commission's decision to visit the South and to accept money from Southern churches, that is churches imbedded in the world of slavery. This decision on the part of the church's commission was, as Richard Blackett terms it, "impolitic" and resulted in a national "send back the money" campaign against the Free Church, designed to force the church to return the money it had gathered from churches associated with slavery. Douglass, alongside fellow abolitionists like George Thompson, played an integral part in the effort to sway public opinion: "to teach their children 'to lisp . . . in the streets when they see a black coat and a white cravat [that is, a clergyman] – SEND BACK THE MONEY' and to paint the slogan on every available wall" (Blackett, *Building an Antislavery Wall*, 90).

In this instance, it is fairly clear that the charges that Douglass is not who he says he is, that he does not have the appropriate credentials, that he is playing on the gullibility of the people, that he is, in other words, an impostor, emanate from a particular political quarter. Douglass successfully implicates opponents of the "send back the money" campaign in the disreputable attempt to stain his unblemished character by accusing him of being an impostor. Thus Douglass is able to turn the attacks against him to his advantage: to link the charges of imposture with an attempt to silence Douglass and to hinder the "send back the money" campaign.[2]

If Douglass's integrity was challenged in part as a way of discrediting his actions and his politics, it is also true that Douglass really was who he had said he was. But charges of imposture were not always so spurious. Indeed, these charges flourished during the African-American abolitionist campaign, and perhaps with good reason. Douglas A. Lorimer suggests, based on a number of remarks in Henry Mayhew's work, that "when the anti-slavery campaign was at its peak, . . . black mendicants were so successful in gaining alms that some English beggars blackened themselves to enhance their appeal" (*Colour*, 41). In other words, the African-American abolitionist campaign was so popular that whites and/or blacks would actually masquerade as fugitive slaves in order to prey on the alms-giving English public.

A notice entitled "Collections in England for the Benefit of American

Slaveholders" which appeared in April 1852 in the *Temperance Chronicle* highlights the dangers of imposture for its readers and some guidelines for dealing with the problem:

When persons representing themselves as fugitive slaves travel as petitioners, we should suggest the propriety of close enquiry into their antecedents. They should be required to produce introductory certificates from well-known friends of the anti-slavery cause, and all collections made on their behalf should be forwarded to some person in Great Britain or Ireland who is willing to act as trustee, and whose name will guarantee that no more than the sum required shall be solicited, and that it shall be fairly appropriated to the object specified. These precautions would protect the public against fraud, and the coloured race and the anti-slavery cause against the odium to which both are subjected when benevolent persons are swindled in their name . . . We cannot too strongly condemn the readiness with which [illegible] and others will admit persons on temperance platforms, without sufficient guarantee that they are worthy of confidence. If they are not the accredited agents of a society, they should have testimonials from respectable and well known individuals.

This notice never actually uses the term "impostor" to label those "persons representing themselves as fugitive slaves" upon whom the notice is casting suspicion. Moreover, since the notice never makes clear whether or not the persons to whom it is calling attention are really fugitive slaves (but instead free blacks from America, free blacks from England, or whites?), it is not easy to determine what about these "persons representing themselves as fugitive slaves" is in question or what exactly constitutes the "fraud" referred to. It's easy, however, to locate the proposed solution. The notice emphasizes that persons travelling for the anti-slavery cause should show themselves to be "worthy of confidence" by demonstrating that they are properly "accredited agents of a society" or by presenting "testimonials from respectable and well known individuals."

Is proper accreditation a way to protect against swindlers? Or could the lack of formal accreditation among travelling lecturers itself be the problem? Given the overwhelming popularity of the African-American abolitionist campaign, fugitive slaves could travel in England without operating under the auspices of the paternalistic organization of the "well-known friends of the anti-slavery cause." Is this fact the source of the fear and discomfort that motivates this notice? Because, of course, without accreditation, without testimonial and sponsorship, a lecturer, authentic or not, would be beholden to no one. He or she could say whatever he or she pleased about slavery, about American society, and about the abolitionist movement, and the only monitor on his or her words would be his or her audiences. Audiences, voting with their feet and their money, and not "well-known friends of the anti-slavery cause," would decide whether or not to validate and support his or her work.

The *Anti-Slavery Advocate* echoes the *Temperance Chronicle* in issuing a call for caution about impostors. In a notice of "Fugitive Slaves on the Tramp in England," the article answers a request for information about a "coloured man named Charles Hill, who has been collecting money . . . for the professed purpose of redeeming his wife from slavery." After a brief discussion of Hill, of whom the paper admits to knowing "nothing," the notice moves from the specific to a general warning against impostors: "we have known of so many persons travelling through the country, and collecting money on false pretenses, that we earnestly recommend all who wish to help the anti-slavery cause, which has been greatly though unjustly disgraced by impostors, to exercise great caution before giving to any unknown person professing to be a fugitive slave." Like the *Temperance Chronicle* above, the *Anti-Slavery Advocate* concedes that "impostors" have been successful in the abolitionist marketplace, in fact, have been able to tell their stories and collect money. Indeed, the notice allows that "so many persons" have been engaged in this practice.

With the *Temperance Chronicle*, then, the notice suggests the necessary response: "Even if he produce satisfactory testimonials from well-known friends of the anti-slavery cause in England or America, he should be required to name a respectable trustee by whom contributions will be received, and who will undertake to appropriate them to the object in view, if any think well to contribute to it." Here, the suggestion is that it is necessary both to verify the authenticity of the speaker (via "satisfactory testimonials") and to monitor the money (with a "respectable trustee"). This solution, however, only underlines the author's desire to dictate the terms of the relationship, especially the financial relationship, between the fugitive slave and his English audiences.

In the hope of establishing such authority over fugitive slaves, the notice continues, arguing: "Fugitive slaves, having obtained the priceless blessing of liberty, should be required to help themselves like other people . . . Let us attack the system, or help those who do, and give none of our money to mendicants of any class without strict inquiry into their character and mode of application." The author of this article in the *Anti-Slavery Advocate* wants to be able to decide when and to whom money

is given. He wants to be able to judge what fugitive slaves need ("liberty") and do not need ("our money"). His paternalism notwithstanding, this notice originates from the fact that what this author wants is not
the case. Charles Hill, of whom the paper knows "nothing," arrived
without testimonials and trustees, but, like "so many persons," he has
been winning the sympathy and the financial support of English audiences.

Charles Hill was actually one name among many for one mysterious
figure who travelled through England, lecturing, collecting money, and
playing a variety of deceptions on the public. Hill appeared under a
variety of aliases, including Henry Smith, Andrew Barker/Baker,
Hiram Swift, William Love, and Reuben Nixon, this last name believed
to be the prominent impostor's own. His is a truly bizarre story. Born a
free man in Albany, New York, Nixon travelled through Ireland and
England, "preaching and lecturing, and collecting large congregations,
and receiving large contributions" ("A Negro Impostor"). He was also
involved in gambling, petty theft, and fraud, and spent three months in
jail in Kewes for crimes of this sort.

On February 6, 1857, the *Montrose, Arbroath and Brechin Review* records
Nixon's visit to Montrose under the name William Love. Speaking in
the "Independent Chapel, Baltic Street (Rev. Mr. Whyte's), which was
crowded in every corner," Love/Nixon told his audience a story of life
in bondage as a valet in the United States. Without any concern or
anxiety over the authenticity of his tale or his identity, the paper records
his visit in an article entitled "American Slavery":

He gave some vivid pictures of the treatment of slaves in general, and on the
different plantations, which included the usual amount of harrowing detail of
the writhing, demoralizing, and brutal effects of the horrid system of American
slavery, which he narrated from his own experience and observation. Some of
his narratives might be regarded as pure fictions or malicious libels on our
American brethren, were they not, alas! corroborated by testimony which
cannot be controverted. The sketches of slave life and character given by Mr.
Love were inimitable, and his impersonations and mimicry were true to life and
most striking as well as amusing; whilst his eloquence and pathos were often
sublime and truly affecting. For nearly two hours did he keep the interest of the
large audience unabated.

The stories of Love/Nixon would only be regarded as "fictions" or
"libels" by those unfamiliar with the "horrid system of American
slavery." The author of the article, like the audience in Montrose, is

confident in his knowledge of that system, presumably by virtue of the wealth of corroborating "testimony" that has passed through Montrose by 1857. In addition to celebrating the accuracy of Love's/Nixon's presentation, the article also emphasizes that his exhibition offers listeners "sublime" amusement. In other words, Love/Nixon was very good at what he did; he told the people of Montrose what they wanted to hear (about the horrors of American slavery), and he did so eloquently and amusingly.

The following week's paper, however, records a very different story about, as the notice puts it, the "fugitive slave from Baltimore, who electrified our citizens by his narration of stirring incidents, his powerful eloquence, and inimitable humour and pleasantry." In an article entitled "Negro Impostor," the *Montrose, Arbroath and Brechin Review* now admits to its readers that "the said William Love, instead of being a fugitive slave, was an accomplished impostor, and had . . . practised the most hollow deceit and imposition." The notice explains that, from documents received, it is clear that Love/Nixon "has never been a slave, except to his inveterate habit of lying and deception; and, though often a fugitive, his flying has only been from those whom he has duped and fleeced. He has a new story for almost every place in which he appears, and a different name for each character he assumes." Hoping that other towns will not fall victim to the same imposition, the article ends with a physical description of Love/Nixon and the warning that his "manners are pleasing, and his voice soft and musical. He can excite great compassion by shedding tears, which he does with great facility."

Another local paper, the *Montrose Standard*, comments on the deception practised by Love/Nixon on the town of Montrose. An article published on February 13, 1857, entitled "A Real Black Man," insists that the "lectures were truly effective . . . and his sincerity was guaranteed by an extraordinary flow of tears." Indeed, this paper explains precisely how complete the deception by Love/Nixon was:

He was received with open arms by some of our ministers and sympathising laymen, and it was regretted that the fashion of this country precluded more than one dinner party per day, otherwise the sable stranger might have been enabled to honour double the number of invitations that were showered upon him. In short, he was regarded as a perfect specimen of all the "moral and Christian virtues bound in black morocco complete" . . . He had ample testimonials in his possession, and he put on the character of the christian and the gentleman with so much plausibility that we do not wonder that some of our most acute ladies and gentlemen were fairly taken in.

There was no *Times* here to warn the unsuspecting or even weak-minded viewer of the unscrupulous deceptions in this exhibit (as had been the case with Stowe's *Uncle Tom's Cabin*). And if the press was taken in, so too were ministers and laymen. Love's/Nixon's possession of "ample testimonials" suggests that leaders in the anti-slavery campaign and in the town itself were persuaded by his stories. Even upon exposure, the *Montrose Standard* cannot condemn the Love/Nixon lectures as "contradictions and absurdities," as had the editor of the *Wolverhampton and Staffordshire Herald* in protecting his gullible readers against Henry "Box" Brown. He had "electrified" his audience; he had appeared a "perfect specimen." Thus even while the notice maintains a generally jocular tone about the incident, the author is forced to conclude with a more serious assessment of the implications of Love's/Nixon's utterly successful imposture: "it argues a culpable degree of gullibility on the part of the public."

A letter to the *Montrose Standard*, published February 21, 1857, addresses the charge of "gullibility" in the "public." Alex Inglis writes that he had read in the *Standard*, "with a kind of humorous smile," the story of Love's/Nixon's imposture

> on the candour and hospitality of some of the leading inhabitants, whose knowledge of the world one would have thought quite sufficient to shield them from impostors. Yet I was not ashamed of Montrose, for the enthusiasm and generous sympathy awakened bespoke hearts alive to the wrongs of downtrodden humanity, and a world-wide charity that rejoiced to alleviate misfortune, and to recognize genuine worth, however humble.

That the town, including its "leading inhabitants" with all their worldly knowledge, were taken in by Love/Nixon is not testament to "a culpable degree of gullibility" for Inglis but to "generous sympathy" and an openness to "genuine worth" that bespeak the superior nature and values of the town's citizens.[3]

Even as Inglis is willing to accept the deception and read it as evidence of the town's all-too-generous, all-too-noble nature, he notes with dismay that the fraud in Montrose was no isolated incident:

> But you could hardly guess my surprise and indignation when, on Sabbath, on my way to church, I observed from bills on the walls that the impostor intended to deliver two lectures in one of the churches in Bathgate. I felt stung with resentment at the trick played off upon my native town, and abomination at the idea of the perpetrator having the audacity to pitch himself directly under my nose, and attempt a repetition of his deception and fraud.

Perhaps because this fraud is attempted in Inglis's own "native town," perhaps because Inglis realizes that he himself might have been subject to and taken in by the charms of Love/Nixon, the "humorous smile" at the story of Montrose's experiences seems to fade. Apparently, Love/ Nixon audaciously measured Bathgate and its "leading inhabitants," such as Inglis, to be equally gullible. Faced with such an assessment of his own town and himself, Inglis was no longer willing to rename "gullibility" as charming "enthusiasm" and felt instead "stung with resentment."

Nixon was not the only impostor to take advantage of the African-American abolitionist campaign in order to perpetrate fraud and deceit.[4] But he was certainly the most notorious. While numerous and continuous warnings like those I discussed above appeared in anti-slavery publications and local newspapers alike,[5] Nixon toured the country and the English people continued to be taken in by this man who could tell tales of the brutality of American slavery and produce tears of pain and sorrow. Reuben Nixon could not be controlled, could not be shut down or shut out; he succeeded over and over again in his imposture because the English crowds kept returning to hear him.

I began this book with the image of John Estlin, pencilling in his "X" marks over Frederick Douglass's words so that his daughter would not read of a slave woman being used as a breeder. For Estlin, this passage in Douglass's text was unnecessary, dangerous to the larger cause of abolitionism, and inappropriate as subject matter for any text. So Estlin, anointing himself the arbiter of what should and should not be read, strikes out the passage in the book. In the process, Estlin takes it upon himself to censor and, in some sense, strives to destroy Douglass's words.

In my initial discussion of Estlin's actions, I noted how bizarrely myopic and ineffective Estlin's censorship of only one passage appeared, given the explicit nature throughout Douglass's volume of his discussion of issues of violence and sexual abuse. Moreover, Estlin's efforts to restrict his daughter from viewing even that one passage in the narrative were actually unsuccessful, since one can make out Douglass's words beneath Estlin's scrawled "X" marks.

Estlin functions like many among the elite of English society who were eager to decide for the disenfranchised new readers/consumers, like his daughter, what they should and should not read. This was true beyond slave narratives. The African-American abolitionist campaign, with its texts from the *Narrative of the Life of Frederick Douglass* to *Uncle Tom's Cabin*, was merely one site on which a national crisis was visible. Over and over again in this book, we have seen the ways in which different members of the Victorian establishment were threatened by the mass consumption of the people and products of American abolition. This consumption was marked by shifts in the reading public resulting in a literary marketplace driven more and more by readers' demands and not by the judgments of intellectual elites. It was also marked by the demand for lectures and exhibitions that were both respectable and entertaining. On a variety of fronts, the Victorian press reacted to this threat by re-casting and re-modelling American abolitionism so that it served English national interests, bolstered English national pride, and secured English national security. So that, in other words, American abolition diffused and contained the very threat that its massive consumption had conjured in the first place. In other words, Mary Estlin's ability to read about a woman as "breeder" in Douglass's narrative and John Estlin's desire to govern his daughter's reading were both symptoms of a larger trend.

As is clear above, however, John Estlin's control, like the control of the Victorian establishment, was never total. African-American abolitionists waged a difficult struggle to retain the integrity of their own voices and of their ideas in the face of a process of cultural absorption in which their identities were appropriated by and amalgamated into an English ideal. Caught in the middle of this cultural crisis, however, individual texts and authors faced an uphill battle against a community eager to fend off the threat they represented.

But the impostor, he who represented himself as a fugitive slave, seems not to have been so easily controlled and contained. Reuben Nixon, for example, took in the masses as well as the elite establishment (the clergy, the leading townspeople, etc.). In his repeated successes, all the worst fears about the African-American abolitionist campaign were realized. His ability to please again and again made demonstrable the ability of the individual Victorian of every class to exercise the right to choose what he or she wished to consume: Nixon's tales. And this choice did not necessarily indicate the individual Victorian's superior national character but perhaps his or her vulnerability to crass and/or immoral culture, or, as the *Montrose Standard* put it, "a culpable degree of gullibility on the part of the public."

The African-American abolitionist campaign made visible a crisis of popular culture and national character that had long been building in Victorian society. That crisis may have also been temporarily contained by the successful wrenching of the campaign to the purpose of preserving an unsullied English national identity. But Reuben Nixon serves as a figure of all that England feared and as a sign that these fears had not been fully dispelled.

Striving to discount and dismiss the circulation of American slave narratives, the *Athenaeum* had warned in a review of *Slave Life in Georgia* that "if the fugitives find a market for their stories, they have a right to deal in them; but we can promise our readers nothing more than the stereotyped account of horrors, and nothing less than sickening amplifications on the effect of the bull-whip and the cobbing-ladle." What this study has shown is that Victorians were indeed queuing up for "the bull-whip and the cobbing-ladle." While that action could be re-interpreted as a measure of a superior noble sympathy on the part of the English nation for those suffering under the pain of American slavery, the fact remains that the English nation was both eager and increasingly free to consume these horrors. And those worrisome facts would outlast the abolitionist campaign.

Notes

1 Mary Estlin's copy of Douglass's *Narrative of the Life of Frederick Douglass*, featuring J. B. Estlin's markings of this passage, is held in the Estlin Papers collection at the Dr. Williams Library in London.

2 See Blackett's examination of the consequences of this international campaign for individual black Americans in *Beating Against the Barriers: The Lives of Six Nineteenth-Century Afro-Americans* and for the transatlantic abolitionist campaign in *Building an Antislavery Wall: Black Americans in the Atlantic Abolitionist Movement, 1830–1860*.

3 See, for example, Rice, *The Scots Abolitionists*; Temperley, *British Antislavery*; Klingberg, *The Anti-Slavery Movement in England*; Craton, *Sinews of Empire*; Walvin, *England, Slaves and Freedom*; and Ferguson, *Subject to Others*.

4 Turley's study leaves two major gaps. First, since he limits his examination to the culture of white English anti-slavery reformers, Turley's study of anti-slavery reform ignores the presence and impact of African-Americans in England and in the white English reform network. Second, while Turley notices the "the quantitative 'popular' aspect of antislavery" (2), his study does not consider the larger consequences of this popularity for English society.

5 On the complications of using the term Englishness versus the term Britishness and of thinking of either entity as both an expression of political dominance and an authentic identity/ethnicity, see C. Hall, *White, Male and Middle Class*, especially pages 25–35; Young, *Colonial Desire*, especially pages 1–6; and Colley, *Britons*, especially pages 5–9.

6 English nationalism pervades the rhetoric of the colonial anti-slavery movement and the world anti-slavery movement. Catherine Hall writes that when England took up the cause of colonial slavery recognizing slavery as a "great national crime" became synonymous with recognizing "what it should mean to be English" (*White, Male and Middle Class*, 27). Only the English could, as a nation, rise above pecuniary interest, face the past, and make appropriate reparations. For further discussion of the historical association of the anti-slavery movement with English nationalism, see Blackburn, *The Overthrow of Colonial Slavery*, 433–46; Turner, *Slaves and*

Missionaries; Temperley, *British Antislavery*; and Turley, *The Culture of English Antislavery*.

I "EXHIBITING UNCLE TOM IN SOME SHAPE OR OTHER"

1 Reviews are listed in the "Primary texts" section of the bibliography, according to the title of the review (if the review was titled); the title of the work reviewed; or, if the review was not titled and is not an explicit review of any one work, under the title of the journal.

2 For helpful bibliographic references to writing about Stowe, see Hildreth, *Harriet Beecher Stowe*, and Jorgenson, *Uncle Tom's Cabin as Book and Legend*. On the anti-slavery but also anti-abolitionist position of the *Spectator* before an abrupt turnabout in policy after the 1858 purchase of the paper by American diplomat Benjamin Moran and American businessman James McHenry, see Fulton, "*The Spectator* in Alien Hands."

3 The *Spectator's* bizarre reading of Stowe's novel as a text of manners and interiors notwithstanding, English interest in American scenery (and in American society generally) was strong and certainly contributed to British interest in *Uncle Tom's Cabin*. See, for example, Bayard Taylor's *Adventures and Life in San Francisco* and Charles Casey's *Two Years on the Farm of Uncle Sam*, the latter a memoir and description of the everyday life and journeys of Casey throughout the United States, one of many such texts published in England to satisfy the curiosity of English readers. Most such texts make at least passing commentary on American slavery, as does Casey who writes that "in this day and generation, it were to be wished by all men that the negro should be allowed to take that place which Nature has organised him for, namely, a servant for hire, not from purchase" (263–4).

4 I am suggesting that *Uncle Tom's Cabin*, and the African-American abolitionist campaign generally, both produced and played into a distinctive moment of cultural flux in Victorian society. A new literary marketplace was emerging in the mid 1840s and early 1850s, the result in part of printing technology and increased literacy. (See, for example, Dalziel, *Popular Fiction 100 Years Ago*.) Stowe's novel was of a piece with the popular literature that would dominate that marketplace. Other cultural institutions, like the music hall and exhibition shows, were undergoing mid-century transformations, in part because anti-slavery politics made these otherwise taboo entertainments respectable and accessible for middle-class audiences. (See Bratton, "English Ethiopians," and Lorimer, "Bibles, Banjoes and Bones.") This cultural shift initiated a crisis; and anxieties, about middle- and lower-class consumption of popular literature and popular entertainment, dominate this period. (See Lorimer, "Bibles, Banjoes and Bones"; Neuberg, *Popular Literature*; Dalziel, *Popular Fiction 100 Years Ago*.) "As the forties drew to a close, the reformers' cry for truly cheap *wholesome* literature grew ever more urgent" (*The English Common Reader*, 287), writes Altick: "people worried about the dangers of moral corruption associated with popular

reading . . . during mid-Victorian times it was uppermost in the minds of those who watched the spread of the reading habit among the masses" (307–8).

5 Altick writes that "*Uncle Tom's Cabin* touched off the biggest sensation the publishing trade had yet known" (*The English Common Reader*, 301). The contribution of the earlier publication and success of American slave narratives to Stowe's sensation is still unexplored territory, although Blackett asserts that the success of American slave narratives in England "in large measure paved the way for *Uncle Tom's Cabin*" (*Building an Antislavery Wall*, 26).

6 The American journal *Putnam's Monthly* would offer another name for the commodification of *Uncle Tom's Cabin* in an article with that same title: "Uncle Tomitudes." Dix, in his *Transatlantic Tracings*, would propose to "Tom-itudinize a little about [Stowe's] books" (70).

7 In a related discussion of English reviews of *Uncle Tom's Cabin*, Lorimer argues that Stowe's text "conveyed, in a more popular form, and with a new vividness, the life and character of Negro slaves in the United States, and thereby aroused English sympathies for their plight. At the same time, it heightened English awareness of the differences between themselves and the black characters of the novel. These differences the mid-Victorians attributed both to the influence of slavery and the effect of race" ("Bibles, Banjoes and Bones," 38). While I find Lorimer's argument appealing, I find his exclusive focus on the relationship between the reception of *Uncle Tom's Cabin* and English racial attitudes misses the complexity of *Uncle Tom's Cabin*'s interaction with Victorian society. See also Gossett, *Uncle Tom's Cabin and American Culture*, for a discussion of the reaction to the novel in the North and South of the United States, England, and the continent.

8 As with so much in Victorian society, our understanding of events is limited by the scarcity of records from the working class and women in contrast to the preponderance of material detailing the opinions of middle-class men. Recourse to working-class newspapers does not necessarily remedy this situation. For instance, a review of Stowe's novel in the working-class and Chartist *People's Paper* reveals little because the paper takes a decidedly non-middle-class approach to its survey of literature: "we shall not follow the plan, so generally adopted, of giving brief, desultory and discursive extracts from the works of others, and overwhelming the page with editorial criticism; but we shall present, abridged and condensed, a complete outline of the work, and leave it principally to the reader to pass his own judgment on the merits and demerits of the author" ("A Tale of Slavery").

9 See Fulton for a discussion of *The Times* as "the most important newspaper in Great Britain" which "both reflected and influenced public opinion" ("'Now Only *The Times*,'" 48).

10 See also the *Daily News* which does not disparage Stowe's financial and commercial success. The review, in contrast to *The Times*'s, notes that "A sale so large, in two countries, of a book by an author new to fame, is an

event, not only in the literary history of the day, but, considering the theme chosen, of some political significance." The *Daily News*, a more liberal newspaper than *The Times*, features a review of *Uncle Tom's Cabin* noteworthy mainly for the praise it lavishes on Stowe's "art": "There is the minuteness of observation and of structure of Dickens . . . There are the marks of genius about the book . . . the flexible style suggests great literary powers . . . Altogether, it is one of the most remarkable novels of recent times." Interestingly, the review prefers Stowe's novel to the work of Henry "Box" Brown, a fugitive slave who escaped from slavery by having himself shipped north in a box. "Box" Brown is fiercely attacked in this review of Stowe; the review notes that Stowe "is not a refugee or emancipated slave appealing to the hollow and vicious sympathies" and that her "illustrations are not the exaggerations of Box Brown panoramas. She selects no hideous exceptional crimes of individual slaveholders."

11 *The Times's* equation of "woman writer" with "erring beginner," while not merely idiosyncratic, was hardly universal in Victorian society. A review in the *British Army Despatch* (reprinted in the *Liberator*), for example, builds on and embellishes *The Times's* sexist rhetoric ("The Uncle Tom's Cabin Mania"). Several reviews praise Stowe's work, however, particularly as the work of a woman writer: the *Illustrated London News* describes Stowe as "a mind equally tender and energetic, religious and philosophical, deep-searching in its views and far-reaching in its eloquence" and finds "the stamp of truth" (290) upon the novel; the *Prospective Review* claims that "Stowe is one more example of the powers of the female mind [in] the composition of fiction" (492); and the *North British Review* praises "the noble work of a noble woman in a noble cause" and reminds readers "that it was a woman, Elizabeth Heyrick, who wrote the pamphlet that moved the heart of Wilberforce" (235). *Blackwood's Edinburgh Magazine* directly addresses *The Times's* attack on Stowe's "female" weapons (albeit in equally sexist language): "*These* are the weapons, not carnal, but of holy temper, with which Mrs. Stowe would enter upon this warfare; and who shall rebuke her, and say her Nay? Not *we*. We say to her, with a tender recollection that it is a WOMAN of whom we are writing, All hail, thou impersonation of Christian love and purity!" ("Uncle Tom's Cabin," 422).

12 I am uncomfortable with the attempt to generalize about the politics of a paper as diversely produced as *The Times*, and thus I find unconvincing Martin Crawford's suggestion that "*The Times* considered black slavery to be both an affront to man's morality and a barrier to his progress" (*The Anglo-American Crisis*, 54). For the historical background to *The Times's* antagonistic position to abolitionism, see Catherine Hall's discussion of the sympathy in the 1830s on the part of *The Times* for colonial slavery, in *White, Male and Middle Class*, especially pages 271–2. See also Fulton's argument that in the pre-Civil-War period *The Times* is anti-abolitionist, if not always clearly for or against slavery itself: "the paper preferred questions that could be reduced to black and white terms, and the question of slavery in the

United States was a maddening shade of gray. Thus, the newspaper changed its focus from slavery, which few people could agree on, to abolitionism, which many people could agree on: abolitionism was an insidious evil because its adherents were fanatics" ("'Now Only *The Times*,'" 50).

13 "Exeter-hall" was "the acknowledged temple of British philanthropy, the meeting place where social and religious institutions of many different persuasions gathered to discuss and proclaim their plans for the betterment of mankind" (Temperley, *White Dreams, Black Africa*, 1). A representation not just of civilization, Christianity, and overall English superiority, it was also the focus of criticism. Casting it as an icon of telescopic philanthropy after the grotesque failure of the Niger Expedition of 1841, Dickens declared: "It might be laid down as a very good general rule of social and political guidance, that whatever Exeter Hall champions, is the thing by no means to be done" (qtd. in Temperley, *White Dreams, Black Africa*, 166).

14 Comparisons of American slave and English laborer exist in abundance in reviews of *Uncle Tom's Cabin*. For a discussion of the history of competition between colonial black slaves and English white slaves, as well as of the consequent antipathies among the working class to West Indian abolition, see Gallagher, especially pp. 3–36. Although *The Times*'s strategy for dealing with this issue strives to secure the dis-alliance of worker and slave, it also threatens the image of the English nation as a land of unsurpassed freedoms by suggesting that English laborers suffer deeply. To insure, in turn, the image of the English worker and the English nation as surpassingly free, other reviews employ a language of national competition. The *North British Review*'s insistence that "it is totally false that the condition of the slave is not infinitely worse than that of the poorest labourer in England" (255) is shown in bas-relief by the review's closing assurance that "we are actuated by no spirit of hostile rivalry" (258). *Dublin University Magazine* is even more revealing in its resolution that "the English workman . . . is better off . . . not only than the American slaves, but . . . his French, Belgian, or German compeers" (600).

15 Goldstrom writes that "What evidence we have suggests that at least one half of working-class adults could read . . . in the 1830s . . . Over the next two decades, the Register General's figures are ample evidence of a steady rise in literacy. If further evidence is needed we have only to look at the vast increase of books, periodicals and newspapers bought by working-class people" (104).

16 Samuel Wilderspin, principal advocate and organizer of infant education in England, also worried about the "lower ranks." However, Wilderspin placed the burden of responsibility for working-class education on the wealthy. As McCann and Young write in their study of the philanthropist: "A lecture on 'The Amusements of the People of England' led him to castigate the directing classes for their treatment of the people. If the amusements of the common people became brutal and cruel, it was because

they were neglected by the upper classes" (290). Wilderspin himself carried out his responsibilities by, among other things, serving as lecturer and vice-president of the Wakefield Mechanic's Institute which "offered intellectual and moral improvement to all the citizens of Wakefield and its weekly lectures were all on popular and literary subjects [including] in the late 40s concerts of classical music [which] helped to form 'cultivated taste'" (288). Wilderspin, then, exemplifies middle- and upper-class concern about the working class, concern which centered on questions of education and on the importance of popular literature to the attempt to cultivate the worker.

17 *Uncle Tom's Cabin* was associated with a variety of bad popular literature: sensation fiction (the Gothic romance and crime novel) and sentimental, domestic fiction. These, according to Altick, were "the sort of literature favored by a large portion of the audience which the expanding system of elementary education had brought into being. Despite the high-minded efforts of men [such as the men at *The Times*] to improve their tastes, the semiliterate public remained stubbornly faithful to the rousing products of these genres" (*Common*, 293). Altick continues, remarking that "The rate at which sensational fiction was selling around 1850 gave deep concern to all public-spirited citizens" (293), *The Times* here clearly among them. "Some interpreted the phenomenon as proof that popular education did more harm than good; others, more sanguine, maintained that the cure lay in improving education and abolishing the taxes which . . . prevented the dissemination of a higher quality of literature" (293).

18 The Adelphi theater, as Jeanne F. Bedell points out, "was the major London theater specializing in melodrama" (14); the association of *Uncle Tom's Cabin* with the Adelphi and with the degraded genre of melodrama here is unquestionably meant by *The Times* to be uncomplimentary to Stowe's artistry.

19 Reviews of *Uncle Tom's Cabin* are full of anxiety about the conflicting role of novels in the new literary marketplace of the fifties. See, for example, *Dublin University Magazine*, which comments that "it is the chief merit of our modern novels, with rare exceptions, to suffuse the boudoir with a gentle emotion, or to send the electricity of a broad grin through a row of young clerks, who suspend their quills to revel in the distortions of gross caricature" (600–1). "'The History of a Christian Slave,'" as the *Magazine* calls Stowe's novel, is in contrast "a book for earnest, full-grown intellects – a book for the silence of the study and the calmness of reflection" (601). The *British Army Despatch*, in contrast, finds Stowe's novel part and parcel of the degraded popular fiction of the day: "We believe it to possess a certain melo-dramatic power, equal in pathos to the "Green Bushes" at the Adelphi, and in incident to a popular novel something between the style of Eugene Sue and George Reynolds . . . devoid of truth, principle and reality . . . highly mischievous, and detrimental to the interest of mankind" (qtd. in the *Liberator*). *Blackwood's Edinburgh Magazine* also sees the degradation of the modern literary marketplace but

distinguishes Stowe's readers: "It were idle to class among [Stowe's readers] those who read simply to indulge a spurious whimpering sentimentality, or to have a morbid curiosity stimulated and inflamed by the scenes of suffering and horror" (423). In contrast, the *Morning Chronicle* insists that all Stowe's novel has to offer is "a harrowing list of atrocities" of slavery and these "will only be relished by that not very strong-minded portion of the community who are fond of a good cry, and take it occasionally as a luxury." The review continues, making clear that this weak-minded reader is the popular reader, "The stories of suffering and brutality . . . are vivid enough to sink, for a time, into the popular mind." Like *The Times*, the *Morning Chronicle* is more dismayed over the existence of this weak-minded, popular reader than over Stowe's novel. What each of these reviews share, with *The Times*, is an acknowledgment of a large, degraded reading audience served by improper, dangerous popular literature.

20 A review of *Uncle Tom's Cabin* in the *Athenaeum* (May 1852) makes clear how *The Times*'s review shaped and articulated earlier, half-formulated public opinion. Like *The Times*, the *Athenaeum* concerns itself with the effect novels such as *Uncle Tom's Cabin* have on the reader: "The good done by books like this must be questioned. They may awaken, – they may excite, – they may distress, – but the emotions originated by their perusal are apt to be confounded with philanthropic devotion . . . Passion is inflamed – pity is stirred, – but benevolence is left in the dark . . . to exhaust itself by its indignation and by its tears." Taking this rhetoric to its logical conclusion, *The Times* builds on the earlier identification of "books like this" with unhealthy emotional effects to associate these books in turn with political and social anarchy. Moreover, while the *Athenaeum* leaves undiscussed what so-called good books ought to be doing, the subsequent review by *The Times* details the "delicate dealing" of "art that would interpret Truth" while at the same time instructing the reader.

21 As Richard Fulton notes, "contemporary newspapers and periodicals regularly referred to it [*The Times*] as 'the leading journal'" ("'Now Only *The Times*,'" 48).

22 Powerful cultural force that it was, *The Times* did not exhaust the possibilities for how Stowe's text could be used. It is beyond the scope of this chapter to detail all the other ways in which Stowe's text was appropriated into specific British debates in reviews ostensibly devoted to the merits of this novel of American abolition. See, for example, the different focus taken in the review of *Uncle Tom's Cabin* in *Household Words* written jointly by Charles Dickens and Henry Morley which focuses on the condition of the working class in England and on how Americans ought to proceed to create an effective black working class.

23 While the *Eclectic Review* was not dominated by religious books or topics, its quasi-religious, imperialist nature is suggested by the fact that all profits from the periodical were donated to the British and Foreign Bible Society. The *Eclectic Review* was unusual in that it "bestowed more attention on

American literature (indeed, all books by or about Americans) than any other English periodical of the time" (Sullivan, 128). As I argue below, the attention paid to *Uncle Tom's Cabin* betrayed "a condescending curiosity about the culture of the young republic" (Sullivan, 128) that also served to enforce a particular vision of Englishness.

24 On the association of the colonial anti-slavery movement with British nationalism, see C. Hall, Ferguson, Blackburn (especially pages 443–6), Turner, and Turley.

25 Cowper's lines here illustrate the popular misunderstanding of the Mansfield decision. Lord Mansfield did not rule against the institution of slavery itself within England. He ruled merely that slaves, once brought to England, could not be forcibly removed back into the colonial provinces. Brought by their colonial masters to England, black slaves were not automatically freed from slavery. See Fryer, pages 122–6.

26 As is clear in this passage, the idea that colonial slavery was abolished primarily as the result of English humanitarianism flourished in the nineteenth century. While still a contested issue among historians, powerful arguments by C. L. R. James and Eric Williams contend that British colonial abolitionism resulted largely from the fact that colonial slavery had grown economically unprofitable.

27 For other examples which echo the nationalist rhetoric of the *Eclectic Review*, see the *Morning Post*, the *Nonconformist*, the *English Review*, and "American Slavery" in the *Westminster Review*.

28 On the question of whether Victorians were able to use Stowe's novel to further some radical political purpose, see Klingberg, who writes that "There is an overwhelming mass of evidence that the English workingmen, becoming conscious of the value of American propaganda and counter-propaganda, were resolved to bring them to bear upon their own desperate political and economic struggles" (551). Klingberg insists that "By identifying themselves with this antislavery movement, British and American, and constantly calling attention to their own grievances, white laborers believed that they would benefit by the freeing of 4,000,000 American slaves. English antislavery sentiment, the workers believed, was strong enough to carry with it some relief for themselves" (552). Klingberg is here, I believe, more optimistic than the evidence explicitly warrants.

2 ABOLITION AS A "STEP TO REFORM IN OUR KINGDOM"

1 All references to *Uncle Tom in England* are from the London edition of the novel. Several English and American editions of *Uncle Tom in England* were published. The editions vary in terms of title-page illustrations and title-page marginalia, but the texts of all editions seem to be identical. The American edition states on its title page that it is published "from an advance copy from England."

A version of this chapter was presented at the London Seminar for Nineteenth-Century Studies at Birkbeck College, University of London, and at the University of Southampton. I am grateful to audiences at both universities for helpful comments and to Isobel Armstrong and Ken Hirschkop for making the respective arrangements. For patient reading and criticism of this chapter, I am thankful to Claire Berardini, Elise Lemire, Kate Ellis, John Gillis, Donald Gibson, Richard Blackett, and Mark Flynn.

2 A German translation of the novel exists, entitled, *Onkel Tom in England. Fortsetzung von Onkel Tom's Hütte*, which was incorrectly attributed to Thomas Clarkson, probably because "Sclaverei und der Sclavenhandel," an excerpt translated from one of his works, appears in volume II of the edition. This misleading attribution is the only speculation I have encountered with regard to the identity of the author of *Uncle Tom in England*.

3 Wilson identifies August 20 as the exact date on which *Uncle Tom's Cabin* turned in England from "a moderate success into a national sensation" (*Crusader*, 325). And the author of *Uncle Tom in England* claims to have penned the novel in seven days. So the timing of events here is reasonable.

4 Lorimer estimates the sales of *Uncle Tom's Cabin* in both the United Kingdom and the British Empire for the first year at 1.5 million (*Colour*, 82).

5 It is crucial to understand the novel's preoccupation with class as a part of a larger ideological shift in which the middle class was struggling with self-definition. As Morris writes, "In the early decades of the nineteenth century, marginalization by class was still a new and harsh experience; it only became the dominant form of social relation with the seizure and consolidation of hegemonic power by the middle class which brought into being the Victorian social formation" (*Dickens's Class Consciousness*, 5). As the dominant form of social relation, and following the disruption by the French Revolution of the aristocracy and of aristocratic values, the middle class defined itself against the corruption of the aristocracy by asserting the importance of "inner worth" (8) or internal virtue: "the moral virtues of enterprise, diligence, and thrifty sobriety" (6). At the same time as these internal virtues distinguished the middle class from the corrupt aristocracy, the middle class also defined themselves against the working class. To "define and justify bourgeois hegemony," the "myth of divine and economic causation . . . proved to be . . . efficacious" under which "prosperity and respectability were held to be the inevitable outward signs and consequences of inner moral worth" (8). See also Davidoff and Hall, *Family Fortunes*.

6 For a discussion of the ideological traditions on which the novel's treatment of the children is based, including "romance idealism" and "naive empiricism," see McKeon, *The Origins of the English Novel*.

7 See Edelstein who writes that the narratives of Frederick Douglass and others "seemed unrepresentative for several reasons: these fugitives had such special leadership qualities and other outstanding personal characteristics that their very uniqueness belied the claim that they spoke for four million oppressed southern slaves" (*The Refugee*, xv), and thus undermined

the generalizability of their political claims.

8 In *Uncle Tom's Cabin*, lighter-skinned blacks are the superiors (intellectually, morally, and socially) of darker-skinned black characters. This narrative economy is the logical consequence both of Stowe's racism and of the ideology of nineteenth-century American society generally, in which so-called white blood was thought to improve the African. For a fuller discussion of the politics of skin-color in *Uncle Tom's Cabin*, see Yarborough, "Strategies of Black Characterization in *Uncle Tom's Cabin* and the Early Afro-American Novel." In contrast, within the narrative economy of *Uncle Tom in England*, the "whiter" mulattos, Tom and Susan, are identified as intellectually and socially inferior to Rosetta and Marossi, the "full" black children, who are, in turn, more fully rewarded within the narrative. The difference might arise from the slightly different politics of skin-color in England where a discourse of contagion, rather than improvement, signal-led the corruption of slavery but also the contamination of "blackness." Hence mixed-blood characters would be considered more degraded and dangerous than their "pure" counter-parts of either color, all black or all white. For a fascinating discussion of this discourse of contagion, see Meyer, "Colonialism and the Figurative Strategy of *Jane Eyre*."

9 As Morris writes, "If prosperity and respectability were held to be the inevitable outward signs and consequences of inner moral worth, then it followed that those who failed in the competitive struggle to make a living and succeed were morally unfit" (*Dickens's Class Consciousness*, 8).

10 Of course the working classes had their own traditions of education, in trades, in oral culture, and in popular culture, not considered of value by middle-class standards; see E. P. Thompson, *The Making of the English Working Class*. For a related discussion of the ways in which the working class both absorbed and disrupted dominant middle-class values about education, see D. Thompson, *The Chartists*, and Goldstrom, "The Content of Education."

11 For discussion of the relationship between freedom and literacy in the slave narrative, see V. Smith, especially her discussion of Frederick Douglass (*Self-Discovery and Authority*, 20–8). For a related discussion of the political complications of white culture for black slaves, see Gates (*The Signifying Monkey*, 127–69).

12 James Pennington, Frederick Douglass, Henry Highland Garnet, and Solomon Bayley were all American ex-slaves. William Cuffee, also spelled "Cuffay," was an English free-born black and a Chartist; see Fryer, *Staying Power*, 235–46.

13 These are Gustavus Vasa, or Olaudah Equiano, *The Interesting Narrative of the Life of Olaudah Equiano, or Gustavus Vasa, the African, Written by Himself* (1789); J. W. C. Pennington, *The Fugitive Blacksmith*; Frederick Douglass, *Narrative of the Life of Frederick Douglass, an American Slave* (1849). Phillis Wheatley was an American slave and poet whose first book, *Poems on Various Subjects, Religious and Moral*, was published in London in 1773.

14 Roughly, moral-force Chartists advocated self-education, self-improve-ment, and self-enlightenment in pursuit of the goals of equality and suffrage for the working classes. Physical-force Chartists, in contrast, were willing to advocate violence in the hopes of pressuring the middle and upper classes to accede to their demands. Both groups sought, primarily between 1837 and 1848, adoption of the "People's Charter." See Jones, *Languages of Class*.

15 The novel is also misleading in its representation of self-improvement and self-education among Chartists as a thorough submersion in middle-class values and ideas. As Dorothy Thompson writes, Chartists "had in many cases proposals for change and improvement which did not involve the abandonment of cherished customs, and above all did not involve the total relinquishment of control over their own work and environment" (*The Chartists*, 111). Further, Chartists were often "preserving customs and institu-tions which were under attack by the forces [the middle class, for example] making for conformity and respectability in early Victorian Britain" (117).

16 Dick Boreas, in his condemnation of the "hinstitutions," may have been thinking of the 1845 General Enclosure Act which, instead of preserving peasant properties and creating legitimate peasant ownership of land, allowed the enclosure of common land. Obviously, this law was a blow to the peasant farmer and was among the many causes for the general deterioration of peasant culture and life. Notice as well the allusion to Dickens's *Hard Times* (1854), a similar attack on "hinstitutions." As Raymond Williams puts it, "Public commissions, Blue Books, Parliamen-tary legislation - all these, in the world of *Hard Times* – are Gradgrindery" (*Culture and Society*, 106).

17 This description of Dick is in keeping with middle-class observations of Chartists and of the working class more generally. Dorothy Thompson remarks: "To the middle-class observer what predominates is the drunken-ness, brutality and lack of formal moral education" (*The Chartists*, 246).

18 See Gregory, *The French Revolution and the English Novel*; Prickett, *England and the French Revolution*; and Scott, "'Things as They Are.'" In "The Function of Criticism at the Present Time" (1860), Arnold complains about the French Revolution in terms that recall Carlyle's "slower reformation" discussed above: "the mania [in France] for giving an immediate and political and practical application to all these fine ideas of the reason was fatal" (525).

19 Because it was wary of the violence associated with abolitionism, *The Times* tried to have it both ways: to abhor slavery and to criticize attempts to abolish slavery. For a fuller discussion of *The Times*'s complicated attitudes towards slavery, see C. Hall, *White, Male and Middle Class*; Fulton, "'Now Only *The Times*'"; and Crawford, *The Anglo-American Crisis*.

20 The novel's choice of trades for Clarke may be an attempt to justify his particular political views. The term "mechanic" does not determine pre-cisely what kind of trade Clarke worked in but it is worth noting that mechanics, because of "the comparative rarity of their skills . . . were not as

likely to be permanently excluded from employment in their trades as members of overstocked trades like weavers, shoemakers and tailors. Mechanics, therefore, who were active in the high point of Chartism, even those who served terms of imprisonment, were probably able to get work again" (D. Thompson, *The Chartists*, 200).

21 As far as I can tell, in the mid nineteenth century, the nickname "Dick" contained no reference to Richard's genitals. "Dick" did, however, connote the generic man, as in "Tom, Dick, or Harry: any three (or more) representatives of the populace taken at random" (*OED*). Dick Boreas, in other words, stands as the novel's representation of the average, unenlightened working man.

22 "Boreas" in Latin is "North wind," commonly associated with destruction and barbarism. Thus Dick's name may also be a slighting allusion to the preeminent Chartist newspaper, Feargus O'Connor's *Northern Star*.

23 Dorothy Thompson writes that "As a mass movement . . . Chartism declined rapidly after 1848" (*The Chartists*, 299). "[T]he better economic climate which accompanied and followed the Great Exhibition of 1851, the increasing stability of Britain's major industries in that period and the organisations which these conditions allowed to develop among the new industrial workforce," according to Thompson, "account for [Chartism's] decline and death" (330). "[A]lthough it took a decade to die," Thompson observes, "it persisted only as a marginal force in British social history in those years" (329). Cole writes that "After 1848 Chartism was merely a residue" (*Chartist Portraits*, 22).

24 See R. Williams's discussion of the industrial novels (*Culture and Society*, 99–119).

25 Disturbances in Ireland were among the 1848 revolutions which threatened English national identity, if not English material politics (see Boyce, *Nationalism in Ireland*, 170–4). That the novel ignores the question of Ireland and eschews any linkage between the black slave and the Irish (see Gibbons, "Race Against Time"; Curtis, *Apes and Angels* and *Anglo-Saxons and Celts*; and Lebow, *White Britain and Black Ireland*) may indicate the difficulty Ireland posed for the construction of a history of "glorious" England.

26 While historians continue to debate the reasons behind the decline of Chartism, they agree about the effectiveness of police action and the English legal system in squelching the movement. The Newport Rising, for example, illustrates this point: police violence against the Chartists left twenty-two dead and three protesters sentenced to death for their actions in the uprising. See D. Thompson, *The Chartists*, 330–9, 70–87.

27 For further discussion of English attitudes on race, see Lorimer, *Colour*; Bolt, *Victorian Attitudes to Race*; Stepan, *The Idea of Race in Science*; and C. Hall, *White, Male and Middle Class*.

28 As Lorimer writes, this period "saw the birth of scientific racism and a change in English racial attitudes from the humanitarian response of the early nineteenth century to the racialism of the imperialist era at the close of

the Victorian age" (*Colour*, 12–13). See also Brantlinger's exploration of the relationship between the imperialist ideology of mid-century imaginative writing and the more vitriolic jingoism of the late Victorian and Edwardian periods in *Rule of Darkness*.

29 Another historical distortion on the part of the novel, this argument flies in the face of the tense and charged relationship between abolitionism and Chartism. See Gallagher, *The Industrial Reformation of English Fiction*, 3–36; and Fladeland, *Abolitionists and Working-Class Problems*.

30 See, for example, a reading of the American flag in a review of *Slave Life in Georgia* in the *Christian Weekly News*: "The stripes on the American flag are truly more significant than the stars, unless the latter are intended to indicate how ill-starred are the subjects of the stripes."

31 The Crystal Palace might be taken as the paradigmatic moment in the reconstruction of England as a glorious nation in an age of Progress, "an occasion for national pride" (Altick, *The Shows of London*, 456).

32 The comparison of worker and slave in political rhetoric has a long and tempestuous history in England (see Gallagher, *The Industrial Reformation of English Fiction*, 3–35; Cobden, *The White Slaves of England*). The transnational tenor of the comparison in this novel, *American* slaves with *English* workers, however, is more unusual. See two other texts which employ this comparison in order to re-direct sympathy for American slaves back towards the English poor: Coatsworth, *Slavery in England*, and Rymer, *The White Slave*.

33 See a number of other responses to *Uncle Tom's Cabin*, written by Americans (many also published in England), in which discussion about American slavery, in contrast to the English treatment of the working class or laboring poor, forms the basis for a creation of American national identity through competition and comparison with England, thus enacting the ideological work of *Uncle Tom in England* in reverse. *The Mud Cabin* (by Warren Isham), a book "design[ed] . . . to furnish a test by which to estimate the value of the institutions of our own country [America]" (preface), argues that "the character and tendency of *their* [England's] institutions is to produce the evils of which I have spoken, while the character and tendency of *ours* is to destroy the evils . . . In the one case, the evils in question are the spontaneous outgrowth of a vicious system, and in the other, they are but fungous excrescences, which the healthful development of the system itself will shed off" (312). Two works of fiction, *The Cabin and Parlor* (T. B. Randolph) and *Tit for Tat* (Marion Southwood), defend the slow march of American slave reform while criticizing English hypocrisy. The author of *Tit for Tat*, a "lady of New Orleans," as the title page proclaims, explains her motivation for writing her tale of English children chimney-sweeps: "The year of grace, Eighteen Hundred and Fifty-four, will be memorable for England, for the breaking out of the Uncle Tom fever. A chronic ophthalmia overspread the vision of English Humanitarians, who, look at what they might, could see nothing but specks of black. They were haunted by black spectres. In all the races of the Earth, none was worthy of pity unless its color was black. The

Black fever was at its height, when I took it kindly. The English, acclimated to the home disease, caught it from America. I, an American, was infected in England. There is a race of beings, by the initiated, facetiously denominated 'chummies,' which exists only in humane Britain. Outside barbarians call them chimney-sweeps. This race is black, not from blood, but from soot. I beheld the specimens of these crippled, distorted, bleeding bits of humanity, and, at sight, was taken down by a sympathetic fever. In my paroxysms, I would exclaim – 'Oh! ye Dukes and Duchesses! ye Lords and Commons! ye Priests and Laymen! who lift up your hands and let fall your tears at the woes of Uncle Tom, thousands of miles away; heard ye never the wailing cry of the poor "chummy" who weeps daily on your thresholds? Oh! Sutherland House! Oh! Exeter Hall! whose walls reverberate with shrieks for freedom to the African, have ye no echoes for the wretched children who shriek relief from torture on your hearthstones?"' (i–ii).

34 The novel's appropriation of abolition for a middle-class political agenda conflates the range of conservative and radical agendas historically present within the ranks of English abolitionists. For a discussion of one abolitionist whose attitudes on issues of class in England reflected neither the hypocrisy nor the political machinations often perceived behind "telescopic philanthropy," see Tyrrell, *Joseph Sturge* (85–134). For a thorough discussion of the range of relations between English abolitionism and working-class radicalism as well as of the political range within the abolitionist movement, see Turley, *The Culture of English Antislavery*; Hollis, "Anti-Slavery and British Working-class Radicalism"; and Fladeland, "'Our Cause being One and the Same.'"

35 Given the nationalist foundation of the colonial anti-slavery movement and the frequency with which the English stressed their virtue at having initiated the world anti-slavery movement, it is entirely consistent to find English popular rhetoric about anti-slavery, as this novel evidences, turning to American slavery as further ammunition for the construction of a superior Englishness. Of the association of the colonial anti-slavery movement with English nationalism, Catherine Hall writes that the rhetoric of anti-slavery contributed to a "morbid celebration of Englishness": the development of an English national identity which was white, male, and middle-class, and which refused the recognition "that Englishness is an ethnicity" (*White, Male and Middle Class*, 205–6). For further discussion of the colonial anti-slavery movement and the ongoing construction of an English national identity, see Blackburn, *The Overthrow of Colonial Slavery*, especially pages 443–6; Turner, *Slaves and Missionaries*; Turley, *The Culture of English Antislavery*; and Temperley, *White Dreams, Black Africa*.

36 For a generous reading of Stowe's transformation of the narratives of escaped slaves, particularly those of Josiah Henson and Henry Bibb, see Hedrick, *Harriet Beecher Stowe*, 211–13. For a more critical and sardonic reading of the politics of this process, see Ishmael Reed's novel, *Flight to Canada*.

3 "REPETITIOUS ACCOUNTS SO PITEOUS AND SO HARROWING"

1 These are the narratives of Moses Roper, Moses Grandy, Frederick Douglass, Charles Ball, Lewis and Milton Clarke, Zamba, Leonard Black, John Hoseph, J. C. Pennington, William Wells Brown, Revd. J. Asher, Henry "Box" Brown, Josiah Henson, Edmond Kelley, Solomon Northup, John Brown, T. D. Bonner, William and Ellen Craft, James Watkins, and Samuel Ward. For further documentation and discussion of the circulation of slave narratives in England, see C. Taylor, *British and American Abolitionists*; Andrews, *To Tell a Free Story*; Starling, *The Slave Narrative*; and Wilson, *Crusader*.

2 Also listed are the earlier slave narrative, *The Interesting Narrative of the Life of Olaudah Equiano* (1789), William Wells Brown's novel, *Clotel* (1853), and Brown's book of travel writing, *Three Years in Europe* (1852).

3 I have limited my focus here to the publication and circulation of slave narratives written by American ex-slaves. Imaginative writing by blacks and whites about American slavery also circulated widely in England, including *Clotel* and *Three Years in Europe*, by the ex-slave William Wells Brown; *Archy Moore, The White Slave*, by white American historian Richard Hildreth; *Autobiography of a Female Slave*, by white American former slaveholder Mattie Griffiths; *Ida May*, by white American novelist Mary Hayden Pike (alias Mary Langdon); and *Lynch Law: Or, the Life and Adventures of Jonathan Jefferson Whitlaw*, by English novelist Frances Trollope.

4 Abolitionism was a cause always fraught with political complications; see Gallagher, *The Industrial Reformation of English Fiction*; Blackburn, *The Overthrow of Colonial Slavery*; and Walvin, *England, Slaves, and Freedom*.

5 On sensationalism, see also Altick, *Victorian Studies in Scarlett*; Kalikoff, *Murder and Moral Decay*; and Haining, *Sweeney Todd*; on pornography, see McCalmon, *Radical Underworld*; and Webb, "Victorian Erotica."

6 Anti-slavery politics appear to have brought respectability to other entertainment in England, particularly black-face and minstrel shows. J. S. Bratton describes "the transfer of anti-slavery sympathy in Britain to black-face performers" as the factor which "enabled them to appeal . . . to a huge popular audience" ("English Ethiopians," 133). Bratton writes that "The dissenting lower middle classes, the ministers, shop keepers, and respectable ladies who were in some ways the most deprived and repressed cultural group in the land, found it possible to go to minstrel shows" (128), in part because of that transfer of anti-slavery sympathy. Black-face acts and minstrel shows thus became "the only access the *respectable* popular audience had to certain liberating elements of popular entertainment" (original emphasis, 128). No doubt slave narratives enjoyed the same appeal as minstrel shows. The narratives' violence may have offered even more in the way of "liberating popular entertainment," but it was their politics which allowed the respectable to read.

7 "As-told-to" narratives are those written by white English or American editors who transcribed the words of black oral narrators. While many of

the editors speak openly about their roles in the production of these narratives, delineating and delimiting their activities explicitly, the vexed question of authenticity in these texts still raises fundamental problems for historians and critics. As William Andrews writes: "it is not the moral integrity of these editors that is at issue but the linguistic, structural, and tonal integrity of the narratives they produced. Even if an editor faithfully reproduced the facts of a black narrator's life, it was still the editor who decided what to make of these facts, how they should be emphasized, in what order they ought to be presented, and what was extraneous, or germane. . . Editors of early Afro-American autobiography assumed the right to do everything to a dictation from 'improving' its grammar, style, and diction to selecting, arranging, and assigning significance to its factual substance" (*To Tell a Free Story*, 20).

8　The American slave narrative forms a crucial part of African-American literary history and as such has received a large amount of critical attention. The best collections of primary texts are Gates, *The Classic Slave Narratives*; Bontemps, *Great Slave Narratives*; and Andrews, *Six Women's Slave Narratives*. Marion Sterling Wilson performed the ground-breaking scholarship on slave narratives, discovering, documenting and describing the narratives in all their breadth and variety. Wilson's work has been continued by Andrews, who stresses that a history of slave narratives must be grounded in an understanding of the political and historical demands on fugitive slaves during different moments within the American anti-slavery movement. Other literary critics have focused on rhetorical strategies in the slave narratives; here see V. Smith, *Self-Discovery and Authority*, especially pp. 9–43; Stepto, *From Behind the Veil*, especially pp. 3–31; S. Smith, *Where I'm Bound*, especially pages 3–27; Gates, *The Signifying Monkey*, especially pp. 127–69; Foster, *Witnessing Slavery*; Gibson, "Reconciling Public and Private"; C. Davis and Gates, *The Slave's Narrative*; Sekora and Turner, *The Art of the Slave Narrative*; and McDowell and Rampersad, *Slavery and the Literary Imagination*.

9　On the question of the conjunction of violence and voyeuristic pleasure, see Herbert's discussion of the complicated "paradoxical fusions" of a "bondage fantasy" at play in American white audiences' responses to Hiram Powers's *The Greek Slave* ("The Erotics of Purity").

10　The existence of such a class of readers eager to eschew the new wares of the emerging literary market may be gauged in part by the success of Mudie's Select Circulating Library. While critics "inveigh[ed] against [circulating libraries] and their stock . . . emphasiz[ing] the corruption of taste and idleness the libraries fostered" (Griest, *Mudie's Circulating Library*, 9), Mudie's established itself as the "'select' library . . . the antithesis of the 'monster-misery' of earlier years" (11). As Griest writes, Mudie "carefully excluded books for 'moral reasons.' No longer would the head of a Victorian family need to waste his time scanning circulating library works to see whether they were suitable for his daughters . . . The concept expressed by his term 'select' formed the keystone of the arch which supported Mudie's great business" (18). The group of "our readers," which the *Athenaeum* attempts to construct and control, were most likely also Mudie's readers.

11 Dalziel identifies the 1840s as "the beginnings of a [new] literature" and a new literary marketplace: "the mass production of fiction which all but the poorest could afford to buy, of fiction therefore that was popular in the most fundamental way . . . A whole new reading public came into being" (*Popular Fiction 100 Years Ago*, 4).

12 Woolford notices major changes in literary criticism in periodicals in the 1850s: "The critics' conception of their own role, in relation to the poet and in relation to the public, was revolutionized." Woolford writes that "Morality is replaced by 'edification' as the appropriate criterion of literary merit" ("Periodicals and the Practice of Literary Criticism," 133). This change, in which the "critics [were] enrolling themselves as the spokesmen of its [the public's] aesthetic tastes" (115), can be seen as in keeping with the *Athenaeum*'s strategy. As the old role of public judge of morality grows obsolete, the critic attempts to create and fill a new need as arbiter of aesthetic taste.

13 My examination of a range of different kinds of publications suggests that reactions to slave narratives speak to larger cultural issues than any one journal's particularity.

14 An overwhelming emphasis on the violence within slave narratives can be found in the reviews. See, for example, the *Hastings and St. Leonards News* which records that "some of its [*Slave Life in Georgia*'s] scenes are indeed horrible . . . laying before the public eye the full criminality of those engaged in the debasing occupation of enslaving and torturing their fellow creatures." The *Nonconformist* finds Henson's and Wells Brown's narratives display "singular and thrilling relations [including] the dangers, cruelties, and inhuman wrongs, of which these narratives furnish deeply affecting and appalling instances." An advertisement for *Slave Life in Georgia* in the *Anti-Slavery Reporter* emphasizes that the account will detail the "life, sufferings, adventures, and escape" of John Brown. The *Anti-Slavery Advocate* recommends Solomon Northup's narrative as a "thrilling work" detailing the "twelve years [Northup] drank the bitterness of slavery" and recommends John Brown's "terrible life" in which his "sufferings were much aggravated by repeated unsuccessful attempts to escape" as a narrative "even with more than the usual proportion of harsh masters, tortured and degraded slaves, and all the inevitable evils of [slavery with its] cruel laws" (256). The *Empire* insists that "never were scenes more 'horrible and heartrending' presented to the human mind than in this little volume [*Slave Life in Georgia*] . . . a record of terror, loathsomeness, avarice, cruelty, and murder! What wrongs, sufferings, privations, persecutions, and unutterable outrages this volume reveals."

15 See the *Morning Chronicle* which, in a discussion of the genre of slave tales and of Stowe's work in particular, distinguishes the displays of the "iniquities" of slavery from similar violent displays in popular writing. Stowe's "design" in

Uncle Tom's Cabin, the review insists, "was to exhibit slavery in its best and worst aspects . . . not merely to produce popular fiction." The morality of the Victorian literary reader and of the Victorian literary marketplace is actually preserved through this transatlantic literary exchange.

16 Playing on English interest in information about American society generally, as well as curiosity about the horrors of slavery, the *Bond of Brotherhood* quantifies the value of John Brown's narrative: "It is an interesting book, full of incident and information . . . Whoever purchases this book will get a good shilling's worth of interesting information in regard to slave-life." Viewing American society through details of slave-life ensures, in this instance, that the English reader will suffer no jealousy and self-doubt through the comparison of English society with American society.

17 The use of abolitionism to denigrate American society generally in the pursuit of a national competition with the United States is one of the mainstays of English abolitionism. On the association of the colonial anti-slavery movement with English nationalism, see C. Hall, *White, Male and Middle Class*; Ferguson, *Subject to Others*; Blackburn, *The Overthrow of Colonial Slavery*, especially pages 443–6; Turner, *Slaves and Missionaries*; and Turley, *The Culture of English Antislavery*. For a related discussion of American abolitionism in England and America-bashing, see Lorimer, "Bibles, Banjoes and Bones."

18 The "quarantine" of British black seamen and the "kidnapping" of these into American slavery had been a sustaining concern for the English. Pressured by public opinion prior to the circulation of Brown's narrative, Palmerston instructed British consuls to negotiate with individual state governments since the American federal authorities had no power to override Southern state law. These negotiations were only partially successful. See Temperley, *British Antislavery*, especially pages 202–3. See also *Imprisonment of British Seamen: Or, the Sovereign Rule of South Carolina* (1852), also published as *Manuel Pereira: Or, The Sovereign Rule of South Carolina* (1853), a slave narrative variation focusing on the quarantine of English black seamen.

4 "NEGROPHILISM" AND NATIONALISM

1 For background and discussion of other aspects of this mid-Victorian obsession, see Altick, *The Shows of London*; Mayer, "The World on Fire"; Bratton *et al.*, *Acts of Supremacy*; MacKenzie, *Popular Imperialism and the Military* and *Imperialism and Popular Culture*.

2 The literature on the "blacking-up" of minstrels and on the political and social ramifications of English black-face entertainers is vast and rich; see Rehin, "Harlequin Jim Crow"; Walvin, *Black and White*; Pickering, "Mock Blacks and Racial Mockery"; Bratton *et al.*, *Acts of Supremacy*; Bratton, "English Ethiopians"; and Riach, "Blacks and Blackface on the Irish Stage." White itinerant street musicians and white mendicants did "black-

up," perhaps induced by English demand and their savvy identification of the interrelation between English sympathy and "pockets full of money." The historical evidence about white beggars who posed as American blacks and/or fugitive slaves, however, is far from complete. Lorimer writes that "Fugitive slaves were so successful at soliciting handouts in the streets of London that white English beggars began to black themselves" ("Bibles, Banjoes and Bones," 34). Lorimer derives this conclusion from warnings in anti-slavery journals against "coloured impostors who gained charity by claiming to be fugitive slaves." His conclusion is complicated, however, by the fact that questions of the genuineness of identity and concerns over imposture are common throughout Victorian culture and often center around the dissemination of power. Charges of imposture, fed by white abolitionists in positions of authority in the British anti-slavery campaign, offer questions about "real" identity but often betray anxiety surrounding the power of African-Americans to run their own political campaign and the encroachment of those African-Americans on the domain of white men.

3 For more details on the lecture tours and their significance, see Ripley, *The Black Abolitionist Papers*, especially pp. 3–35; Blackett, *Building an Antislavery Wall* and *Beating Against the Barriers*; C. Taylor "Notes on American Negro Reformers"; and Gara, "The Professional Fugitive."

4 See, for example, an article in the *Bradford Observer* entitled "Panorama of Slavery in America" which records the excitement surrounding "Box" Brown's exhibition in Bingley. The notice explains that a "large room at Oddfellows' Hall was crowded to suffocation, and the last night Mr. Brown was obliged, in order to pacify the public, to promise a second performance, which took place at ten o'clock, and at that late hour the room was again filled."

5 Given the fact that no anti-slavery panoramas are known to have survived, it is important to recall that commentary cannot be assumed to be a full and accurate representation of the painting. That said, this lack of information about the panoramas need not hamper an examination of what is at stake in what the commentators did choose to write about and to scrutinize, or of why they might have "seen" what they did on the canvas.

6 See also a notice in the *Leeds Mercury*, the "Horrors of Slavery in America." "Box" Brown's exhibition provides English viewers with a glimpse into the splendor of America: "All persons were highly gratified with the splendid views of American scenery." For all its wealth of splendid scenery, however, admiration for America is abruptly curtailed as all "were horrified on witnessing the curse of slavery as depicted and carried on in the United States." An untitled article in the *Newcastle Chronicle* records interest in "Box" Brown's romantic escape matched by interest in the "life-like delineation of scenes ["of real life in the Slave States"] of which happily in this free country we could otherwise form but a faint idea." Englishmen and women, inhabitants of a "free country," are justly "horrified" at being asked even to conceive of the horrors of slavery.

7 A notice in the *Leeds Mercury* ("The Mirror") gives us some sense of who "Box" Brown's audiences were. The notice reads: "Mr. Brown, on Thursday evening, announced a reduction of his charges for admission; and stated that the scholars and teachers in Sunday schools would be admitted by special arrangement." A reduction in the admissions price indicates that "Box" Brown's exhibition attracted different segments of the British public: groups (different classes, to speak generally) with differing abilities to pay. It was common practice in Victorian society at this time to have reduced admission prices at specified performances of an exhibition. (The Great Exhibition had such a policy of price reductions, for example.) That way the "respectable" classes could attend the more expensive showing without worrying about contact with the "lower" classes.

8 See, in contrast, a notice of recommendation for "Box" Brown in the *Leeds Mercury* ("The Mirror"). The notice explains that "Box" Brown's "panorama of American slavery, was painted for him by three of the first artists of [Boston] . . . Since his arrival in England, he has exhibited his panorama at Liverpool, Manchester, and other places. It is exceedingly well painted, and both as a work of art, and as conveying to the mind vivid representations of slavery in every form, well merits the attention of the public." The fact that "vivid representations of slavery" really do "merit" the attention of the public is attested to by a judge with proper institutional authority: a Reverend. The notice insists, "The Rev. Andrew Lynn, of the Methodist New Connexion was present, and stated that at Bradford the exhibition had given the greatest satisfaction; and from personal interviews with Mr. Brown, and other information, he believed his object was to enlighten the people of this country as to the horrors of American slavery." Thus even though the panorama might have provided its audiences with titillation, given its munificence of "modes of capturing, flogging, torturing, and branding," the commentary is able to describe it as acceptable moral entertainment, in part by stressing its artistic merit and in part by stressing its moral project.

9 See also Bratton, "English Ethiopians," for a discussion of the limited access of respectable audiences to popular entertainment and theater in England.

10 Little is known about this Mrs. "Box" Brown.

11 That lecturing blacks might become a racist spectacle, appealing to other than anti-slavery impulses in their audiences, was a concern throughout the African-American abolitionist campaign. A letter from J. B. Estlin to the white American abolitionist Samuel May expresses this concern: "The Crafts have been with us for the most part of 3 weeks . . . They had kind but not judicious, (& some vulgar) advisers in the North of England, neither their interest nor *respectability* (Ellen's espy) being properly consulted. Some of their hand-bills have been headed 'Arrival of 3 Fugitive Slaves from America'!! as if 3 monkeys had been imported, and their public appearance has been too often of the *exhibitive* kind. Neither B. nor, of course Craft, was

quite *up* to the sort of position they ought to take, Ellen's *instincts* made her view the whole matter in its precisely correct light" (qtd. in C. Taylor, *British and American Abolitionists*, 377–8).

12 Two notices about "Box" Brown's exhibition in the *Preston Guardian and Advertiser* illustrate the complexity of English consumption of these spectacles. "Box" Brown's exhibition is recommended to the "religious public" and to children; the "teachers of St. John's Sunday School" proclaim, in the newspaper, that the exhibition "is calculated to leave a lasting impression upon the mind, and particularly that of the young" (Untitled, Jan. 25). Whatever the "impression" of the exhibition is understood by the teachers to be, it apparently coexists unproblematically with a brief vignette, in an earlier issue of the same paper. Entitled "Negro Rivalry," the vignette reads: "By cash, Pompey," said Sambo, "you should see what I hab bought: such a splendacious particular walking stick – him so bery fine, him nearly walk alone." "What the debil wodnerful about dat, Massa Sambo," replied Pompey. "I can tell you I hab got at home a black tea-pot what *runs*" (Jan. 18). For further discussion of British racism and of the question of whether exhibitions such as "Box" Brown's and negro minstrelsy exacerbated English racism, see Rehin, "Harlequin Jim Crow"; Bratton, "English Ethiopians"; Pickering, "Mock Blacks and Racial Mockery"; and Lorimer, "Bibles, Banjoes and Bones" and *Colour*.

13 Remond pursued her education while in England, attending Bedford College for Ladies in 1859 and 1860. In 1866, she went to Florence, Italy, where she became a doctor and married. She lived out her life in Italy, practicing medicine. For further biographical information on Remond, see Ripley, *The Black Abolitionist Papers*, and Bogin, "Sarah Parker Remond."

14 On the occasion of her appearance in Warrington, the *Warrington Standard* records that: "The hall was filled, nay, 'twas crammed to suffocation, and every square foot of the room was occupied. Indeed, the crush interfered sadly with our reporter, for he was unable to make his way through the throng to the platform, so he had to report as best he could among the body of the audience. The crowd outside was very great, and many people who came to the door in carriages had to return disappointed. The doors too had to be locked, in order to prevent the people outside from further incommoding the audience" ("Lecture on American Slavery"). The *Warrington Times* offers the common solution to such over-crowding: tickets, meant to price out the poor from attendance. Noting that "Great numbers of most respectable people were thus debarred entrance," the *Warrington Times* suggests: "We think that the gentlemen making the arrangements would have acted more wisely had they issued tickets, and thus have secured a few seats for the better class of people who were almost entirely excluded, or a small charge would have effected the same object" ("Lecture on American Slavery"). This procedure was immediately adopted, and admission was charged for the assembly. The *Warrington Guardian* reports: "As the lectures at Liverpool and Warrington were delivered without charge for admission, the inhabitants of Penketh have

the satisfaction of feeling that they are the first in England to contribute pecuniary aid to this zealous advocate of negro emancipation" ("District News"). The make-up of Remond's audiences correspondingly shifted to "an intelligent and respectable audience in the Day School Room" ("District News"), "a fashionable and numerous attendance" ("Miss Remond's Second Lecture on Slavery"), and "a highly respectable audience" ("American Slavery," *Manchester Weekly Times*).

15 Victorians clearly appreciated the differences between Remond and "Box" Brown. See, for example, the *Warrington Guardian* which praises Remond's manner in unspoken distinction from showmen like "Box" Brown: "The calm and deliberate appeal to the understanding of her auditors without any attempt to captivate the imagination by a detail of the horrors of the slaveholding system, proves that she possesses powers of eloquence of a high order" ("District News").

16 See also Thomis and Grimmett, who write of "the unease felt at the unaccustomed female presence in the political arena" (*Women in Protest*, 26).

17 The Mayor's speech is recorded slightly differently in the *Warrington Standard*: "The Mayor in his opening address, briefly touched on the fact, that women [in England] did not take that part in public matters that they did in America, but he did not see why it should be so, for he did not see anything indecorous in a lady addressing an audience" ("Miss Remond's second lecture on Slavery"). In this rendition of the speech, the Mayor seems to endorse the practice of having female lecturers. However, his suggestion that having such a practice is not "indecorous" makes clear that the standard public argument about such matters is that female lecturers are indeed indecorous. The Mayor, whatever his view on the subject, clearly associates the American nation with this controversial practice. See also the *Liverpool Mercury* which defends Remond's position: "women, without at all feeling that they sacrificed their womanhood, appeared on the public stage to rehearse a fictitious tragedy, [hence] there was no reason why a woman should not speak in public of a real tragedy, and on a subject upon which she so deeply felt" ("A Lady Lecturing"). However, for many middle-class women, to appear on a theatrical stage would mean the sacrifice of one's womanhood. The "alleged immorality of actresses was . . . notorious" (Booth, *Theater in the Victorian Age*, 22) during this period and formed a large component of the hostility towards theater generally. For this reason, the comparison between Remond and female actors suggests a lingering misgiving about female "performers."

18 Readers may here recognize the foundation for Toni Morrison's *Beloved*.

19 See also Remond's discussion recorded in the *Warrington Guardian* on the sexual abuse of female slaves in slavery: she "described a slave sale, and said that when they [slave women] were exposed for sale, their persons were not always covered. The more Anglo-Saxon blood that coursed in their veins the more gold they would fetch. These were sold to be the concubines of the white Americans, and not to be plantation slaves" ("Miss Remond's Lec-

ture"). For a discussion of Remond's specific contributions on women's issues, see Ware, *Beyond the Pale*.

20 See McCaskill's related discussion of how Ellen Craft was "'exhibited' to British Victorian sentiments in the service of abolition." McCaskill shares many of my concerns and notices the same dynamic in the English consumption of Ellen Craft: "Silent, demure, Ellen . . . enhanced the abolitionists' tactics of transmuting her identity racially and sexually from sullied quadroon slave to civilized, authentic 'white' lady" ("'Yours Very Truly,'" 523). I disagree, however, with McCaskill's optimistic conclusion that Craft, and other black American abolitionists, were successful in manipulating "the spectacle of their bodies to be forceful ammunition against slavery" (525).

21 The *Warrington Times* describes Remond's lecturing abilities in similar terms: "her gentle and easy manner, combined with an animated and intelligent countenance, rivets the attention of her auditors . . . her thoughts is [*sic*] oftentimes not of an ordinary character, and, spoken with a pure accent, and in the voice of a fine modulating nature . . . she is often eloquent and thrilling" ("Lecture on American Slavery," Jan. 29). The *Bolton Chronicle* also adds Remond's appearance to her feminine attributes: "the lecturer . . . is a young and good-looking woman, of prepossessing countenance, fluent speech, and ladylike demeanour" ("Lecture on American Slavery, by a Lady of Colour"). See also the *Manchester Weekly Times* which expresses approval that Remond's lectures are "modestly and nobly advocated" ("American Slavery").

22 One interesting chapter in the story of Remond's activities in England concerns her speeches to ladies' groups, and the coverage of those events continues the work of constructing Remond as an honorary member of a white, English sisterhood. At one event, the presentation of a watch to Remond from a Warrington Ladies' organization, "Miss Remond addressed about forty ladies in the Assembly Room of the Lion Hotel [who] presented her with a watch, bearing a suitable inscription. Miss Remond attempted to acknowledge the compliment, but her feelings so overcame her that she could do little more than shed tears" ("Miss Remond's Morning Lecture"). Other accounts, however, record more than Remond's tears and use this occasion to reflect on Remond's position in English society. The *Warrington Standard* records that "Miss Remond, who was deeply affected, said that for the first time in her life had she been removed from the pressure there always was upon people of colour in America; and every hour she had spent in England had been happiness to her, for she had felt none of that objection to her which existed in the United States because of her race" ("Lecture on American Slavery"). The *Warrington Times* makes the ideological move most plainly: Miss Remond responded to the testimonial saying, "I do not need this testimonial. I have been received here as a sister by white women for the first time in my life. I have been removed from the degradation which overhangs all persons of my complexion and I

have felt most deeply since I have been . . . in England that I have received a sympathy I never was offered before." The *Warrington Times* also proudly notes that "Mrs. Ashton . . . addressing [Remond] in a few most affection-ate sentiments, said she felt proud to acknowledge her as a sister" ("The Lecture at the Lion Hotel"). The costs of this white sisterhood, however, are also in evidence in these accounts. See, for example, the *Warrington Guardian* which includes the following remarks at the end of an article on "Slavery and Democracy" supposedly inspired by Remond's visit: "Had the meeting consisted of blacks, they no doubt would have proposed a vote of thanks to him in the language used at a coloured dinner party . . . 'Here's to the gubbernor; tho' him got a white face, him hab a black heart!' (Cheers, and cries of, 'Long lib massa, the gubbernor.')" Remond's acceptance as a "white" sister seems to have had absolutely no effect on general attitudes about black inferiority.

23 See also an article in the *Warrington Times* entitled "The Slave Trade": "American slavery is the lowest and the worst form of [despotism] that ever existed in the world, and this measures the atrocity of intensity of the despotism that upholds it. The liberties of the world are not safe so long as such a huge power as that wielded by the American republic is concen-trated upon the enslavement of an entire race of mankind. The first step of all moral progress is ceasing to do evil. There can be no moral progress for the world so long as the Cabinet of North America is in the hands of the slaveholders."

24 Karen Jean Hunt is in the process of writing a biography of Remond where she discusses an incident in which Remond manipulated the English press in a tussle over a visa. Hunt's reading of this incident allows her to conclude that Remond was a savvy, sophisticated person well versed in the mechan-isms of politics and what we now call public relations. This incident notwithstanding, I am less optimistic, not about Remond's personal skills, but about her individual agency in the larger Victorian field.

EPILOGUE

1 I presented material from this chapter at the Northeast Victorian Studies Association conference at Villanova and at the New England Historical Association conference at Amherst College. I am grateful for the feedback from participants at both conferences, and, in particular, the thoughtful commentary of Howard Wach at the latter.

2 For further discussion of Douglass's involvement in the "send back the money" campaign, see Blackett, *Building an Antislavery Wall*, pages 79–117.

3 After listening to this material at the Northeast Victorian Studies Associ-ation conference at Villanova, a member of the audience made the interest-ing suggestion that "Inglis" might be a clever pseudonym/homonym for "English," that is, the average Englishman.

4 See, for example, an untitled article in the *Liverpool Mercury* which records

the conviction and imprisonment of a "negro, calling himself the Rev. Alfred Thomas Wood, DD," sentenced to eighteen months' hard labor. Wood, the paper states, had "been going about in this country and in Ireland during the greater part of last year, collecting subscriptions professedly for completing a new church in Monrovia, in the republic of Liberia ... He had represented himself in different places as an episcopalian, an independent, and a baptist, according to circumstances."

5 For other warnings about or discussions of Nixon, see, for example, the following: "Caution" in the *Brighton Examiner* and "Negro Impostor" in the *Windsor and Eton Express*.

Bibliography

PRIMARY TEXTS

Adams, F[rancis] C[olburn]. *Imprisonment of British Seamen: Or, the Sovereign Rule of South Carolina*. London: Clarke, Beeton, and Co., 1852.

Manuel Pereira: Or, The Sovereign Rule of South Carolina. London: Clarke, Beeton, and Co., 1853.

"American Slavery." *Manchester Courier and Lancashire Advertiser*, September 17, 1859 (vol. 35, no. 1999): 9.

"American Slavery." *Manchester Daily Examiner and Times*, September 15, 1859 (no. 1426): 3.

"American Slavery." *Manchester Weekly Times*, September 17, 1859 (no. 92): 5.

"American Slavery." *Montrose, Arbroath and Brechin Review*, February 6, 1857.

"American Slavery." *Warrington Guardian*, February 5, 1859, supplement (no. 221): 2.

"American Slavery." *Warrington Guardian*, February 12, 1859, supplement (no. 222): 4.

"American Slavery and Emancipation by the Free States." *Westminster Review*, January 1, 1853 (vol. 59, no. 115): 125–67.

"American Slavery and 'Uncle Tom.'" *North British Review*, November 1852 (vol. 18, no. 35): 235–58.

Andrews, William L., ed. *Six Women's Slave Narratives*. New York: Oxford University Press, 1988.

"Anti-Slavery Meeting." *Banner of Ulster*, December 26, 1845.

Untitled. *Anti-Slavery Reporter*, January 1860 (vol. 8, no. 1): 16.

Arnold, Matthew. *Culture and Anarchy*. Ed. J. Dover Wilson. Cambridge University Press, 1932.

"The Function of Criticism at the Present Time." *Victorian Poetry and Poetics*. Ed. Walter E. Houghton and G. Robert Stange. Boston: Houghton Mifflin, 1968: 522–35.

Rev. of *Autobiography of a Fugitive Negro*, by Samuel Ringgold Ward. *Anti-Slavery Advocate*, January 1, 1856 (no. 40): 325.

Bontemps, Arna, ed. *Great Slave Narratives*. Boston: Beacon Press, 1969.

"British and Foreign Anti-Slavery Society." *Anti-Slavery Reporter*, June 2, 1851 (vol. 6, no. 66): 85.

Brown, John. *Slave Life in Georgia*. Ed. F. N. Boney. (London, 1855) Savannah: The Beehive Press, 1972.

Carlyle, Thomas. *Selected Works, Reminiscences and Letters*. Cambridge, MA: Harvard University Press, 1970.

Casey, Charles. *Two Years on the Farm of Uncle Sam. With Sketches of his Location, Nephews, and Prospects*. London: Bentley, 1852.

Catalogue of New and Standard Works in Circulation at Mudie's Select Library. November 1857.

Catalogue of New and Standard Works in Circulation at Mudie's Select Library. July 1858.

"Caution." *Brighton Examiner*, February 14, 1854.

Coatsworth, J. *Slavery in England, Or A Picture of the Many Hardships Endured by Our Fellow Countrymen in their Several Stations of Life*. London: E. Marlborough, 1860.

Cobden, John C. *The White Slaves of England*. Buffalo, NY: Derby, Orton and Mulligan, 1853.

"Collections in England for the Benefit of American Slaveholders." *Temperance Chronicle*, April 1852.

"Contemporary Literature of America." *Westminster Review*, January 1853 (vol. 59, no. 3): 287–302.

Dickens, Charles, and Henry Morley. "North American Slavery." Rev. of *Uncle Tom's Cabin*, by Harriet Beecher Stowe. *Household Words*, September 18, 1852 (no. 130): 1–6.

"District News." *Warrington Guardian*, January 29, 1859 (no. 320): 5.

Dix, John Ross [Phillips, George Spencer]. *Transatlantic Tracings: Or, Sketches of Persons and Scenes in America*. London: W. Tweedie, 1853.

Douglass, Frederick. *Narrative of the Life of Frederick Douglass, an American Slave*. (London: 1845) New York: Penguin, 1982.

"English Negrophilism." *Anti-Slavery Standard*, July 1, 1847 (vol. 7, no 5): 17.

Estlin, J. B. Letter to J. Otis, Bristol, November 5, 1845. American Anti-Slavery Society Papers. (MsA 9.2 vol. 21, pages 87–8) Boston Public Library.

Ferguson, Moira, ed. *The History of Mary Prince: A West Indian Slave*. (London, 1831) London: Pandora Press, 1987.

"Fugitive Slaves on the Tramp in England." *Anti-Slavery Advocate*, August 1853: 85.

Gates, Henry Louis, Jr., ed. *The Classic Slave Narratives*. New York: New American Library, 1987.

Griffiths, Mattie. *Autobiography of a Female Slave*. (1857) New York: Negro University Press, 1969.

Hildreth, Richard. *Archy Moore, The White Slave*. (1856) New York: Negro University Press, 1969.

"Horrors of Slavery in America." *Leeds Mercury*, May 3, 1851: 10.

Inglis, Alex. Letter. *Montrose Standard*, February 21, 1857.

Isham, Warren. *The Mud Cabin: Or, the Character and Tendency of British Institutions, as Illustrated in their Effect Upon Human Character and Destiny*. New York: D. Appleton and Co., 1853.

"The Ladies' Meeting." *Warrington Standard*, February 5, 1859 (no. 36): 4.

"A Lady Lecturing on American Slavery." *The Liverpool Mercury*, January 22, 1859 (vol. 49, no. 3412): 4.

Langdon, Mary. *Ida May*. London: Sampson and Low, 1854.

"The Lecture at the Lion Hotel." *Warrington Times*, February 5, 1859 (no. 5): 4.

"Lecture on American Slavery by a Coloured Lady." *Warrington Times*, January 29, 1859 (no. 4): 1.

"Lecture on American Slavery, by A Lady of Colour." *Bolton Chronicle*, October 1, 1859 (vol. 35, no. 1821).

"Lecture on American Slavery by a Lady of Colour." *Warrington Standard*, January 29, 1859 (no. 35): 4.

"Leeds Temperance Union." *Leeds and West Riding Express*, December 31, 1859 (vol. 2, no. 107): 3.

Untitled. *Liverpool Mercury*, January 11, 1853 (vol. 43, no. 2466): 23.

"The Mirror of American Slavery." *Leeds Mercury*, May 24, 1851: 5.

"Miss Remond's First Lecture in Dublin." *Anti-Slavery Advocate*, April 1859 (no. 28, vol. 2).

"Miss Remond's Lecture." *Warrington Guardian*, January 29, 1859, supplement (no. 320): 1.

"Miss Remond's Morning Lecture." *Warrington Guardian*, February 5, 1859, supplement (no. 221): 2.

"Miss Remond's Second Lecture on Slavery." *Warrington Standard*, February 5, 1859 (no. 36): 4.

Rev. of *The Narrative of William W. Brown*, by William Wells Brown. *North and South Shields Gazette*, December 14, 1849.

Rev. of *The Narrative of William W. Brown*, by William Wells Brown, and of *The Life of Josiah Henson*, by Josiah Henson. *Nonconformist*, August 20, 1851 (vol. 9, no. 301): 673.

"A Negro Impostor." *Brighton Herald*, March 18, 1854 (no. 2504): 3.

"Negro Impostor." *Montrose, Arbroath and Brechin Review*, February 13, 1857.

"Negro Impostor." *Windsor and Eton Express*, July 15, 1854 (vol. 43, no. 2190).

"Negro Rivalry." *Preston Guardian and Advertiser*, January 11, 1851.

Untitled. *Newcastle Chronicle*, October 15, 1852: 6.

"The 'Nigger' Panorama." *Wolverhampton and Staffordshire Herald*, March 24, 1852.

Onkel Tom in England. Fortsetzung von Onkel Tom's Hütte. Leipzig: O. Wigond, 1853.

"Panorama of Slavery in America." *Bradford Observer*, May 1, 1851.

Peabody, Ephraim. "Narratives of Fugitive Slaves." *Christian Examiner*, 47 (July 1849): 61–93.

Untitled. *Preston Guardian and Advertiser*, January 18, 1851: 5.

Untitled. *Preston Guardian and Advertiser*, January 25, 1851.

Randolph, T. B. [Peterson, Charles Jacob]. *The Cabin and the Parlor: Or, Slaves and Masters*. Philadelphia: T. B. Peterson; London: Clarke, Beeton and Co., 1852.

"A Real Black Man." *Montrose Standard*, February 13, 1857.

Ripley, C. Peter, ed. *The Black Abolitionist Papers*. Vol. II. *The British Isles, 1830–1865*. Chapel Hill: University of North Carolina Press, 1985.

Rymer, James. *The White Slave: A Romance for the Nineteenth Century*. London: E. Lloyd, 1844.

[Senior, Nassau W.]. "Slavery in the United States." *Edinburgh Review*, April 1855 (vol. 101, no. 206): 293–331.

Advert. for *Slave Life in Georgia*, by John Brown. *Anti-Slavery Reporter*, October 1854 (vol. 2, no. 10): 240.

Rev. of *Slave Life in Georgia*, by John Brown. *Anti-Slavery Advocate*, April 1855 (no. 31): 256–7.

Rev. of *Slave Life in Georgia*, by John Brown. *Athenaeum*, March 31, 1855 (no. 1431): 378.

Rev. of *Slave Life in Georgia*, by John Brown. *Banner of Ulster*, June 30, 1855 (vol. 14, no. 1455): 4.

Rev. of *Slave Life in Georgia*, by John Brown. *Bond of Brotherhood*, March 1855 (no. 56): 127.

Rev. of *Slave Life in Georgia*, by John Brown. *British Friend*, March 1, 1855 (no. 3, vol. 13): 76.

Rev. of *Slave Life in Georgia*, by John Brown. *Christian Weekly News*, February 27, 1855 (vol. 2, no. 35): 140.

Rev. of *Slave Life in Georgia*, by John Brown. *Eclectic Review*, May 1855 (vol. 9): 624.

Rev. of *Slave Life in Georgia*, by John Brown. *Empire*, February 24, 1855 (no. 69): 202.

Rev. of *Slave Life in Georgia*, by John Brown. *Hastings and St. Leonards News*, March 16, 1855.

Rev. of *Slave Life in Georgia*, by John Brown. *Herald of Peace*, May 1855 (no. 59): 204.

Rev. of *Slave Life in Georgia*, by John Brown. *John O'Groat's Journal and Weekly Advertiser*, June 29, 1855 (no. 972): 4.

Rev. of *Slave Life in Georgia*, by John Brown. *Local Preachers' Magazine and Christian Family Record*, June 1855: 231.

Rev. of *Slave Life in Georgia*, by John Brown. *Morning Chronicle*, April 14, 1855: 7.

Rev. of *Slave Life in Georgia*, by John Brown. *Scottish Press*, March 30, 1855: 6.

Rev. of *Slave Life in Georgia*, by John Brown. *Wesleyan Times*, March 19, 1855 (vol. 7, no. 340): 179–80.

"The Slave Trade." *Warrington Times*, February 19, 1859 (no. 7): 4.

"Slavery and Democracy." *Warrington Guardian*, February 5, 1859, supplement (no. 221): 2.

[Southwood, Marion]. *Tit for Tat: A Novel by a Lady of New Orleans*. London: Clarke, Beeton and Co., 1854.

Stowe, Harriet Beecher. *Uncle Tom's Cabin, or, Life among the Lowly*. (New York, 1852) New York: Penguin, 1986.

"Summer Assizes." *The Times*, July 30, 1852: 6e–f.

"A Tale of Slavery." *People's Paper*, August 28, 1852 (no. 17): 6.

Taylor, Bayard. *Adventures and Life in San Francisco*. London: Bentley, 1852.

"The Theatres." *Spectator*, December 4, 1852 (no. 1275): 1159–60.

"To the Editor of the Warrington Guardian." *Warrington Guardian,* January 22, 1859 (no. 319): 4.

Trollope, Frances. *Lynch Law; Or, The Life and Adventures of Jonathan Jefferson Whitlaw*. London: Ward and Lock, 1857.

Uncle Tom in England; Or, A Proof that Black's White. London: Houlston and Stoneman; New York: A. D. Failing, 1852.

Rev. of *Uncle Tom in England*. *Athenaeum*, October 2, 1852 (no. 1301): 1056.

Rev. of *Uncle Tom in England*. *Spectator*, Sepember 18, 1852 (no. 1264): 904.

"Uncle Tomitudes." *Putnam's Monthly,* January 1853 (vol. 1): 87–102.

"Uncle Tom's Cabin." *Blackwood's Edinburgh Magazine*, October 1853 (vol. 74, no. 256): 391–423.

"Uncle Tom's Cabin." *English Review*, October 1852 (vol. 18, no. 35): 80–115.

"Uncle Tom's Cabin." *Morning Chronicle*, September 16, 1852: 3.

"Uncle Tom's Cabin." *Nonconformist*, September 8, 1852: 707–9.

"Uncle Tom's Cabin." *Spectator*, September 25, 1852 (no. 1265): 926–8.

"Uncle Tom's Cabin." *The Times*, September 3, 1852: 5.

Rev. of *Uncle Tom's Cabin*, by Harriet Beecher Stowe. *Athenaeum*, May 22, 1852: (no. 1282): 574.

Rev. of *Uncle Tom's Cabin*, by Harriet Beecher Stowe. *Christian Observer*, October 1852 (no. 178): 695–712.

Rev. of *Uncle Tom's Cabin*, by Harriet Beecher Stowe. *Daily News*, August 4, 1852 (no. 1935): 2.

Rev. of *Uncle Tom's Cabin*, by Harriet Beecher Stowe. *Dublin University Magazine*, November 1852 (vol. 40, no. 139): 600–13.

Rev. of *Uncle Tom's Cabin*, by Harriet Beecher Stowe. *Eclectic Review*, December 1852: 717–44.

Rev. of *Uncle Tom's Cabin*, by Harriet Beecher Stowe. *Illustrated London News*, October 2, 1852, supplement (vol. 21): 290–1.

Rev. of *Uncle Tom's Cabin*, by Harriet Beecher Stowe. *Morning Post*, September 10, 1852 (no. 24,562): 7.

Rev. of *Uncle Tom's Cabin*, by Harriet Beecher Stowe. *Prospective Review*, 1852 (vol. 8, no. 32): 490–513.

The Uncle Tom's Cabin Almanack Or Abolitionist Memento. London: John Cassell, 1853.

"The Uncle Tom's Cabin Mania." *Liberator,* January 21, 1853 (vol. 23, no. 3): 1.

Untitled. *West London Observer*, March 12, 1859.

Untitled. *Wolverhampton and Staffordshire Herald*, March 17, 1852.

Wright, John P. *An Historical Parallel between the Anti-Vivisection Movement in England and the Anti-Slavery Movement in America*. (Publication information unknown, held at Dr. Williams Library, London, England.) *c.* 1854.

Yellin, Jean Fagan, ed. *Incidents in the Life of a Slave Girl*. (Boston, MA, 1861) Cambridge, MA: Harvard University Press, 1987.

SECONDARY TEXTS

Altick, Richard. *Deadly Encounters: Two Victorian Sensations.* Philadelphia: University of Pennsylvania Press, 1986.

The English Common Reader: A Social History of the Mass Reading Public, 1800–1900. University of Chicago Press, 1957.

The Shows of London. Cambridge, MA: Harvard University Press, 1978.

Victorian Studies in Scarlet. New York: W. W. Norton and Co., 1970.

Andrews, William L. *To Tell a Free Story: The First Century of Afro-American Autobiography, 1760–1865.* Chicago: University of Illinois Press, 1988.

Baker, Houston A. *Workings of the Spirit: The Poetics of Afro-American Women's Writing.* University of Chicago Press, 1991.

Bedell, Jeanne F. "Wilkie Collins." *Twelve Englishmen of Mystery.* Ed. Earl F. Bargainnier. Bowling Green, OH: Bowling Green University Press, 1984: 9–32.

Best, Geoffrey. *Mid-Victorian Britain.* New York: Shockew Books, 1972.

Birdoff, Harry. *The World's Greatest Hit: Uncle Tom's Cabin.* New York: S. F. Vanni, 1947.

Blackburn, Robin. *The Overthrow of Colonial Slavery, 1776–1848.* London: Verso, 1988.

Blackett, R. J. M. *Beating Against the Barriers: The Lives of Six Nineteenth-Century Afro-Americans.* Ithaca: Cornell University Press, 1986.

Building an Antislavery Wall: Black Americans in the Atlantic Abolitionist Movement, 1830–1860. Ithaca: Cornell University Press, 1983.

Blassingame, John W. "Black Autobiographies as History and Literature." *Black Scholar,* 5 (1974): 2–9.

Bogin, Ruth. "Sarah Parker Remond: Black Abolitionist from Salem." *Essex Institute Historical Collections,* 110.2 (April 1974): 120–50.

Bolt, Christine. *Victorian Attitudes to Race.* London: Routledge and Kegan Paul, 1971.

Booth, Michael R. *Theater in the Victorian Age.* New York: Cambridge University Press, 1991.

Boyce, D. George. *Nationalism in Ireland.* Baltimore: Johns Hopkins University Press, 1982.

Brantlinger, Patrick. *Rule of Darkness: British Literature and Imperialism, 1830–1914.* Ithaca: Cornell University Press, 1988.

Bratton, J. S. "English Ethiopians: British Audiences and Black-Face Acts, 1835–1865." *Yearbook of English Studies,* vol. 2 (1981). *Literature and its Audience:* 127–42.

Bratton, J. S., ed. *Music Hall: Performance and Style.* Philadelphia: Open University Press, 1986.

Bratton, J. S., Richard Allen Cave, Breandan Gregory, Heidi J. Holder, and Michael Pickering. *Acts of Supremacy: The British Empire and the Stage, 1790–1930.* Manchester University Press, 1991.

Cole, G. D. H. *Chartist Portraits.* London: Macmillan, 1941.

Colley, Linda. *Britons: Forging the Nation, 1707–1837.* New Haven: Yale University Press, 1992.

Craton, Michael. *Sinews of Empire: A Short History of British Slavery.* Garden City, NY: Anchor Books, 1974.

Crawford, Martin. *The Anglo-American Crisis of the Mid-Nineteenth Century: The Times and America, 1850–1862.* Athens: University of Georgia Press, 1987.

Curtis, L. Perry, Jr. *Anglo-Saxons and Celts: A Study of Anti-Irish Prejudice in Victorian England.* University of Bridgeport, 1968.

Apes and Angels: The Irishman in Victorian Caricature. Washington: Smithsonian Institution Press, 1971.

Dalziel, Margaret. *Popular Fiction 100 Years Ago: An Unexplored Tract of Literary History.* London: Cohen and West, 1957.

Davidoff, Leonore and Catherine Hall. *Family Fortunes: Men and Women of the English Middle Class, 1780–1850.* University of Chicago Press, 1987.

Davis, Charles T., and Henry Louis Gates, Jr. *The Slave's Narrative: Texts and Contexts.* New York: Oxford University Press, 1984.

Davis, David B. *The Problem of Slavery in the Age of Western Revolution, 1770–1823.* Ithaca, NY: Cornell University Press, 1975.

Drescher, Seymour. *Capitalism and Antislavery: British Mobilization in Comparative Perspective.* London: Macmillan, 1986.

Edelstein, Tilden G. Introduction. *The Refugee: A North-Side View of Slavery.* By Benjamin Drew. Reading, MA: Addison Wesley Publishing, 1969: ix–xxviii.

Ferguson, Moira. *Subject to Others: British Women Writers and Colonial Slavery, 1670–1834.* New York: Routledge, 1992.

Ffrench, Yvonne. *The Great Exhibition: 1851.* London: Harvill Press, 1950.

Fladeland, Betty. *Abolitionists and Working-Class Problems in the Age of Industrialization.* Baton Rouge: Louisiana State University Press, 1984.

"'Our Cause being One and the Same': Abolitionists and Chartism." *Slavery and British Society*: Ed. James Walvin: 69–99.

Foster, Frances Smith. *Witnessing Slavery: The Development of Ante-bellum Slave Narratives.* Westport, CT: Greenwood Press, 1979.

Fox-Genovese, Elizabeth. *Within the Plantation Household: Black and White Women of the Old South.* Chapel Hill: University of North Carolina Press, 1988.

Fryer, Peter. *Staying Power: The History of Black People in Britain.* London: Pluto Press, 1984.

Fulton, Richard D. "'Now Only *The Times*, is on our Side': The London *Times*, and America before the Civil War." *Victorian Review*, 16.1 (Summer 1990): 48–58.

"*The Spectator* in Alien Hands." *Victorian Periodicals Review*, 24.4 (Winter 1991): 187–96.

Gallagher, Catherine. *The Industrial Reformation of English Fiction: Social Discourse and Narrative Form: 1832–1867.* University of Chicago Press, 1985.

Gara, Larry. "The Professional Fugitive in the Abolition Movement." *Wisconsin Magazine of History*, 48.1 (Autumn 1964): 196–204.

Gates, Henry Louis, Jr. *The Signifying Monkey: A Theory of Afro-American Literary Criticism.* New York: Oxford University Press, 1988.

Genovese, Eugene D. *Roll, Jordan, Roll: The World the Slaves Made.* New York: Vintage Books, 1976.

Gibbons, Luke. "Race Against Time: Racial Discourse and Irish History." *Oxford Literary Review*, 13.1–2 (1991): 95–117.

Gibson, Donald B. "Reconciling Public and Private: Frederick Douglass's Narrative." *American Literature*, 57 (1985): 549–69.

Goldstrom, J. M. "The Content of Education and the Socialization of the Working-class Child 1830–1860." *Popular Education in the Nineteenth Century.* Ed. Phillip McCann. London: Methuen, 1977: 93–110.

Gossett, Thomas F. *Uncle Tom's Cabin and American Culture.* Dallas: Southern Methodist University Press, 1985.

Gregory, Allene. *The French Revolution and the English Novel.* Port Washington, NY: Kennikat Press, 1915.

Griest, Guinevere L. *Mudie's Circulating Library and the Victorian Novel.* Bloomington: Indiana University Press, 1970.

Haining, Peter. *Sweeney Todd: The Demon Barber of Fleet Street.* London: Frederick Muller Limited, 1979.

Hall, Catherine. *White, Male and Middle Class: Explorations in Feminism and History.* Cambridge: Polity Press, 1992.

Hall, Stuart. *Culture and the State.* Popular Culture: U203. Milton Keynes: Open University Press, 1982.

Hedrick, Joan D. *Harriet Beecher Stowe: A Life.* New York: Oxford University Press, 1994.

Heller, Tamar. *Dead Secrets: Wilkie Collins and the Female Gothic.* New Haven: Yale University Press, 1992.

Herbert, T. Walter, Jr. "The Erotics of Purity: *The Marble Faun*, and the Victorian Construction of Sexuality." *Representations*, 36 (Fall 1991): 114–32.

Hildreth, Margaret Holbrook. *Harriet Beecher Stowe: A Bibliography.* Hamden, CT: Archon Books, 1976.

Hollis, Patricia. "Anti-Slavery and British Working-class Radicalism in the Years of Reform." *Anti-Slavery, Religion, and Reform: Essays in Memory of Roger Anstey.* Ed. Christine Bolt and Seymour Drescher. Hamden, CT: Archon, 1980: 294–315.

James, C. L. R. *The Black Jacobins.* London: Secker and Warburg, 1938.

James, Louis. *English Popular Literature: 1819–1851.* New York: Columbia University Press, 1976.

Johnson, Richard. "Educational Policy and Social Control in Early Victorian England." *Past and Present*, 49 (November 1970): 96–119.

Jones, Gareth Stedman. *Languages of Class: Studies in English Working Class History, 1832–1982.* New York: Cambridge University Press, 1983.

Jorgenson, Chester E. *Uncle Tom's Cabin as Book and Legend: A Guide to the Exhibition.* The Friends of the Detroit Public Library, 1952.

Kalikoff, Beth. *Murder and Moral Decay in Victorian Popular Literature.* Ann Arbor: UMI Research Press, 1986.

Klingberg, Frank J. *Anti-Slavery Movement in England: A Study in Humanitarianism.* New Haven: Yale University Press, 1968.

———. "Harriet Beecher Stowe and Social Reform in England." *American Historical Review*, 43.3 (April 1938): 542–52.

Lebow, Richard Ned. *White Britain and Black Ireland: The Influence of Stereotypes on Colonial Policy.* Philadelphia: Institute for the Study of Human Issues, 1976.

Legman, G. *Love and Death, A Study in Censorship.* New York: Hacker Art Books, 1963.

Levine, Lawrence. *Black Culture and Consciousness: Afro-American Folk Thought from Slavery to Freedom.* New York: Oxford University Press, 1977.

Lorimer, Douglas A. "Bibles, Banjoes and Bones: Images of the Negro in the Popular Culture of Victorian England." *In Search of the Visible Past: History Lectures at Wilfred Laurier University, 1973–1974.* Ed. Barry M. Gough. Waterloo, Ontario: Wilfred Laurier University Press, 1975: 31–50.

———. *Colour, Class, and the Victorians: English Attitudes to the Negro in the Mid-nineteenth Century.* London: Leicester University Press, 1978.

MacKenzie, John, M., ed. *Imperialism and Popular Culture.* Manchester University Press, 1986.

———. *Popular Imperialism and the Military, 1850–1950.* Manchester University Press, 1992.

Marchand, Leslie A. *The Athenaeum: A Mirror of Victorian Culture.* Chapel Hill: The University of North Carolina Press, 1941.

Mayer, David. "The World on Fire . . . Pyrodramas at Belle Vue Gardens, Manchester, c. 1850–1950." *Popular Imperialism and the Military.* Ed. MacKenzie: 179–97.

McCalmon, Iain. *Radical Underworld: Prophets, Revolutionaries and Pornographers in London, 1795–1840.* Cambridge University Press, 1988.

McCann, Phillip, and Francis A. Young. *Samuel Wilderspin and the Infant School Movement.* London: Croom Helm, 1982.

McCaskill, Barbara. "'Yours Very Truly': Ellen Craft – The Fugitive as Text and Artifact." *African-American Review*, 28.4 (Winter 1994): 509–29.

McDowell, Deborah E., and Arnold Rampersad, eds. *Slavery and the Literary Imagination.* Baltimore: The Johns Hopkins University Press, 1989.

McKeon, Michael. *The Origins of the English Novel, 1600–1740.* Baltimore: The Johns Hopkins University Press, 1987.

Meyer, Susan L. "Colonialism and the Figurative Strategy of *Jane Eyre.*" *Victorian Studies*, 34.1 (Winter 1990): 247–68.

Midgley, Clare. *Women against Slavery: The British Campaigns, 1780–1870.* London: Routledge, 1992.

Morris, Pam. *Dickens's Class Consciousness: A Marginal View.* New York: St. Martin's Press, 1991.

Neuberg, Victor E. *Popular Literature: A History and Guide.* London: The Woburn Press, 1977.

Nichols, Charles H. "Who Read the Slave Narratives?" *Phylon Quarterly*, 20.2 (Summer 1959): 149–62.

Pickering, Michael. "Mock Blacks and Racial Mockery: The 'Nigger' Minstrel and British Imperialism." *Acts of Supremacy*. Ed. Bratton *et al*: 179–236.

Prickett, Stephen. *England and the French Revolution*. Houndmills: Macmillan Education, 1989.

Reed, Ishmael. *Flight to Canada*. New York: Random House, 1976.

Rehin, George F. "Harlequin Jim Crow: Continuity and Convergence in Blackface Clowning." *Journal of Popular Culture*, 9.3 (Winter 1975): 682–701.

Riach, Douglas C. "Blacks and Blackface on the Irish Stage, 1830–60." *Journal of American Studies*, 7.3 (1973): 231–41.

Rice, Duncan C. *The Scots Abolitionists 1833–1861*. Baton Rouge: Louisiana State University Press, 1981.

Scott, Iain Robertson. "'Things As They Are': The Literary Response to the French Revolution, 1789–1815." *Britain and the French Revolution, 1789–1815*. Ed. H. T. Dickinson. New York: St. Martin's Press, 1989: 229–49.

Sekora, John, and Darwin Turner. *The Art of the Slave Narrative: Original Essays in Criticism and Theory*. Macomb: Western Illinois University Press, 1982.

Slosson, Preston William. *The Decline of the Chartist Movement*. New York: AMS Press, 1968.

Smith, Sidonie. *Where I'm Bound: Patterns of Slavery and Freedom in Black American Autobiography*. Westport, CT: Greenwood Press, 1974.

Smith, Valerie. *Self-Discovery and Authority in Afro-American Narrative*. Cambridge, MA: Harvard University Press, 1987.

Starling, Marion Wilson. *The Slave Narrative: Its Place in History*. Boston: G. K. Hall and Co., 1981.

Stepan, Nancy. *The Idea of Race in Science: Great Britain, 1800–1960*. Hamden, CT: Archon Books, 1982.

Stepto, Robert B. *From Behind the Veil: A Study of Afro-American Narrative*. Chicago: University of Illinois Press, 1979.

Sullivan, Alvin, ed. *British Literary Magazines: The Romantic Age, 1789–1836*. Westport, CT: Greenwood Press, 1983.

Taylor, Barbara. *Eve and the New Jerusalem: Socialism and Feminism in the Nineteenth Century*. London: Virago, 1983.

Taylor, Clare. *British and American Abolitionists. An Episode in Transatlantic Understanding*. Edinburgh University Press, 1974.

"Notes on American Negro Reformers in Victorian Britain." *British Association for American Studies*, 2 (March 1961): 40–51.

Temperley, Howard. *British Antislavery, 1833–1870*. Columbia: University of South Carolina Press, 1972.

White Dreams, Black Africa: The Antislavery Expedition to the River Niger, 1841–1842. New Haven: Yale University Press, 1991.

Terry, R. C. *Victorian Popular Fiction, 1860–80*. Atlantic Highlands, NJ: Humanities Press, 1983.

Thomis, Malcolm I., and Jennifer Grimmett. *Women in Protest 1800–1850*. New York: St. Martin's Press, 1982.

Thompson, Dorothy. *The Chartists: Popular Politics in the Industrial Revolution*. New York: Pantheon Books, 1984.

Thompson, E. P. *The Making of the English Working Class*. New York: Penguin Books, 1963.

Turley, David. *The Culture of English Antislavery, 1780–1860*. New York: Routledge, 1991.

Turner, Mary. *Slaves and Missionaries: The Disintegration of Jamaican Slave Society, 1787–1834*. Chicago: University of Illinois Press, 1982.

Tyrrell, Alex. *Joseph Sturge and the Moral Radical Party in Early Victorian Britain*. London: Christopher Helm, 1987.

Walvin, James. *Black and White: The Negro and English Society, 1555–1945*. London: The Penguin Press, 1973.

England, Slaves, and Freedom, 1776–1838. Jackson: University Press of Mississippi, 1986.

Walvin, James, ed. *Slavery and British Society, 1776–1846*. London: Macmillan Press, 1982.

Ware, Vron. *Beyond the Pale: White Women, Racism, and History*. New York: Verso, 1992.

Watson, Colin. *Snobbery with Violence: Crime Stories and Their Audience*. New York: St. Martin's Press, 1971.

Webb, Peter. "Victorian Erotica." *The Sexual Dimension in Literature*. Ed. Alan Bold. London: Vision Press, 1982: 90–121.

Weiner, Martin J. *English Culture and the Decline of the Industrial Spirit, 1850–1980*. New York: Cambridge University Press, 1981.

Williams, Eric. *Capitalism and Slavery*. New York: Capricorn Books, 1966.

Williams, Raymond. *Culture and Society, 1780–1950*. New York: Penguin Books, 1962.

Wilson, Forrest. *Crusader in Crinoline: The Life of Harriet Beecher Stowe*. New York: J. B. Lippincott Company, 1941.

Wood, Marcus. "Uncle Tom in England: The Publishing Piracy and Influence of *Uncle Tom's Cabin*, in Britain, 1852–1900." *Publishing History*, 32 (1992): 83–4.

Woolford, John. "Periodicals and the Practice of Literary Criticism, 1855–64." *The Victorian Periodical Press: Samplings and Soundings*. Ed. Joanne Shattock and Michael Wolff. University of Toronto Press, 1982: 109–44.

Yarborough, Richard. "Strategies of Black Characterization in *Uncle Tom's Cabin*, and the Early Afro-American Novel." *New Essays on Uncle Tom's Cabin*. Ed. Eric J. Sundquist. New York: Cambridge University Press, 1986: 45–84.

Young, Robert J. C. *Colonial Desire: Hybridity in Theory, Culture and Race*. New York: Routledge, 1995.

Index

Lightning Source UK Ltd.
Milton Keynes UK
07 November 2009
145916UK00001B/82/P